Bark Less Wag More

How to Simplify the Complicated Everyday Life

Suzette Brawner and Jill Brawner Jones

Contents

Introduction

I read once you aren't a real empty nester until all the kids are gone *and* the dog dies. Our fourteen-year-old black Labrador retriever had to be put down when Jill was ten years old. Josie was a part of our family before Jill was. A week later, Jim and Jill came home from their only-to-look-at-puppies trip holding Sally, a 6-week-old chocolate Lab. At fifteen, Sally died and we haven't tried to replace her. I guess I officially fit into the empty nester category.

My first dog was Emma. Emma was a mixed-breed stray my granddaddy had found. My brother and I named her after my grandmother. It only seemed appropriate. Emma was such a patient dog and tolerated us dressing her up in doll clothes and parading her around in a wagon. Without complaining she would fill in as characters in backyard theatrical productions. The next summer Emma was visited by the neighborhood Romeo and we were blessed with four puppies. We learned a lot about life and responsibility from Emma and her babies.

One Sunday afternoon when the pups were still fresh, we went to see my grandparents who lived about an hour away. On the way home we ran into a torrential rainstorm. Mom was worried about the puppies and for a good reason. To escape the August heat, Emma had dug a little cave under the concrete base of the air conditioner to give birth. Mom knew they would drown if Emma couldn't get them out.

7

Finally at home, we ran to the back yard hoping for the best, but dreading what we might find. I'll never forget Mom in the pouring rain down on her knees in the mud with a flashlight. What we saw was something I'll always remember.

Water was quickly filling up Emma's birthing room, however she had done some rearranging. This mother had lined up the babies in front of her. She started at one end of the row and, with her nose, lifted each of their tiny noses up out of the water ... 1, 2, 3, 4, then started over again 1, 2, 3, 4. The little white dog instinctively knew in the time it took to carry one pup to safety, the others would drown. We could almost feel Emma's relief when she saw Mom. If dogs talked she surely would have said, "Wow, am I glad to see you."

We learned something that day. Dogs know things.

Honestly, we humans know things too, but we're too distracted to pay attention. Life is just too complicated, it seems. But really we choose to make it that way. With all the texts, tweets, calls and email we find ourselves connected but scrambling to establish relationships. If we would just slow down, look up, and become a little more intentional, we might see some changes begin.

Jill and I want this book to be a glimpse of hope, a gift of encouragement and a reminder life is too short to not enjoy. God's lessons about life, love, gratefulness, friendships, forgiveness and faith are first found in scripture then lived out before us every day in, sometimes, the most unlikely places. Our part is to be willing to notice.

Let's be inspired,

Suzette Brawner

Chapter 1

If You Want Your Dreams To Come True, Wake Up And Go To Work

"Today is your day.   Your mountain is waiting so...get on your way!"

-Dr. Seuss

I have been accused of being overly social. I will admit I have a tendency to talk to random strangers because I find people so intriguing. Some of the best conversations have been at Starbucks. It's a country club of sorts. Only serious coffee drinkers join, membership is about $4.00-a-day and you can meet the most fascinating people.

One day I decided to go to the serious coffee drinkers country club for a Grande Soy Chi Latte and thumb through a magazine. Standing in line, I spotted a family with adorable identical twin baby boys. I love babies and think it was God's greatest idea; starting people off as babies all fresh, innocent and unaware. Most of the time they're satisfied to just hang out. Life is pretty simple from their perspective since everyone does everything for them.

As I was adding sugar to my drink, one of the little guys caught my eye. I flashed him a big goofy grin and he laughed so hard he almost choked. His parents looked over at me to see what was so funny. They both smiled and the mother said "Our boys are learning early the importance of flirting."

We struck up a conversation so they asked me to join them. I was grateful because they were sitting in the section with the big fluffy couch and the over stuffed chair. During a few minutes of polite chatting we discovered we attended churches down the street from each other. The conversation moved to spiritual things and stories of life journeys.

After talking for a while I began to feel like an unintentional life coach. From what I understand, life coach is the title for someone who you meet with like a psychologist or therapist to learn how to get your life together. I think life coaches sound awesome. My friend in her late 30's had spent thousands of dollars on therapy trying to figure out why she was so depressed and could never get a date. A mutual friend of ours suggested a life coach. After three sessions she is very happy and married to a really wonderful guy.

. . . .

From what I understand, life coach is the title for someone who you meet with like a psychologist or therapist to learn how to get your life together.

. . . .

That was miraculous to me so I asked her what she had learned from the coach. She explained even though she only had three sessions, her coach was like a chiropractor of the heart. "It was as if she knew exactly what to adjust and zeroed in on it."

She broke it down in to three things. Lesson one: Ask all of your friends to set you up on blind dates. This is much better than trying to meet a man at a bar. Your friends know you and have your best interest in mind. Lesson two: Quit feeling sorry for yourself. Lesson three: Forgive those who have hurt you and move on. Brilliant!

So attempting to life coach was what I found myself in the middle of.

Chad and Sarah had been married ten years. They had trouble conceiving and spent enough to buy a new car on fertility drugs and procedures. Finally the last chance method worked and they conceived twins! Six months after discovering she was pregnant, Chad's company down sized and he lost his job. Because of the delicate nature of her pregnancy Sarah was put on bed rest so she had to quit her job. They already knew it was most economical for her to stay home with the boys anyway since childcare for two newborns would be very costly.

As I listened to details of their journey, I began to feel sorry for them. It had been rough, I'm sure. "So Chad, what are you doing now?" I casually asked.

"Oh, I'm still out of work. It's been almost two years since I lost my job and it's been a real struggle. We have eaten through our savings and we refinanced our house twice," he answered with a furrow in his brow.

"Yikes, no luck finding a job, huh?", I asked thinking two years with two babies and a high-risk pregnancy must have run up some kind of a medical bill. That alone gave me a headache.

"Oh no, I've had several job offers, but none of them have been just right. I'm really just holding out for a management position with benefits and good pay," he said matter-of-factly.

I couldn't believe what I was hearing! Holding out for a management position! Come on! At first I thought he was joking.

"Sarah, what about you? Could Chad stay home with the kids while you took a job? Didn't you say you have a law degree?" I asked trying to come up with a solution like it was my own problem.

"Oh, we are really more comfortable with traditional roles. We know God's got a perfect job lined up for Chad. We are just waiting on the Lord," she answered with a smile.

"Unbelievable!", I thought as I headed to the door saying good-bye realizing I had failed my try-out session as an accidental life coach.

What is this? Sometimes I think my generation needs someone to come along and jerk the slack out. Maybe if we lined up and had a little man run by smacking everyone telling us to wake up and get off our fannies there might be some change. But I'm not sure.

• •

What is this? Sometimes I think my generation needs someone to come along and jerk the slack out.

• •

Spike White was like a bonus Grandpa in my life. He was one of the wisest, most loving men I've ever known. His life mission was to serve people. He literally laid the foundation for what is now the world's largest Christian sports camp, Kanakuk. He lived by the creed, "Work like it all depends on you, and pray like it all depends on God." Since I had just met Chad and Sarah in Starbucks, I didn't feel like I had earned the right to share Spike's wisdom with them, but that's what they really needed to hear.

God honors those who are in motion. We need to be willing to do our part by turning on and moving forward. He has promised to lead and guide us down the best pathway for our lives, but frankly if we are in park He's not going to be leading us anywhere. There is no need to steer a parked car.

It seems everyone today is searching for his or her purpose. Each one of us was put on this earth for a specific reason. Just considering the amazing odds of the egg and sperm uniting to make you validates that. Have you ever been told you are one in a million? You're more like one in 400 million! Psalm 139: 15 confirms that God didn't second-guess Himself after He put you here. "My frame was not hidden from you when I was made in the secret place. When I was woven together in the depths of the earth, your eyes saw my unformed body." There is an absolute reason for you because God is a God of order.

Why do we float through life waiting for everything to come to us? We need to go after it. Have you ever written a personal mission statement? Most successful companies have a mission statement so why shouldn't we. The point is to list your goals and lay out a plan. Then the most important step is to take action. You have to remember there is usually a large chunk of time between the initial plan and the point when you see it all come together. The dream part is not so hard. What's difficult is understanding work has to follow. When you hear about an overnight success, don't believe it. Generally many years of behind the scenes sweat equity has been invested.

. . . .

When you hear about an overnight success, don't believe it.
Generally many years of behind the scenes sweat equity has
been invested.

. . . .

The future is shaped by the choices we make today. Do you have a plan and are you willing to get up and work the plan? Why do we all feel so entitled? A recent college graduate may have a plan to own his own company, but what he really needs to have is perseverance. I believe my generation wants what our parents and grandparents have, but we don't want to work and wait for it, we want it now. So instead of accepting a job that might not meet all the criteria as perfect, like Chad, many turn down amazing opportunities. The road to a dream is rarely a straight one. There are many turns and detours, but it is all a part of the journey to gather wisdom to be able to handle yourself when you do reach your destination. The bottom line is; you are the only one who can put your dreams into motion. So get up and go!

Maybe the problem is that my generation just doesn't know how to roll up their sleeves and go to work or they might just be holding out for a management position. During the Great Depression I doubt many people were talking about how unfulfilling their jobs were. I think most were just grateful to have a job. This generation, called the "Builders", can teach us something about diligence and commitment while the next generation, the "Boomers", can show us how to persevere no matter our beginnings. We need to learn from the generations before us. We call it flipping burgers now. They called it an opportunity then. We need to get over thinking we are entitled without putting in the effort.

14

In Los Angeles there is a burger joint that has been in business since the 1940's. Over the years Apple Pan has seen a huge transformation in the landscape around it's original building. However, what goes on inside has virtually remained unchanged. Customers walk through a screen door into a U shaped dining bar. Everything operates on the honor system. You wait your turn for a seat at the bar. There is only a limited menu; hamburgers, chicken salad sandwiches, famous French fries and pies that melt in your mouth. There is a sign on the wall that's probably the reason behind their long-standing success. It reads: *Apple Pan–Doing Simple Things Exceedingly Well.*

That must be the key. Even if you are doing simple things, do them exceedingly well. Martin Luther King Jr. is quoted saying,

"If a man is called to be a street sweeper, he should sweep streets even as Michelangelo painted, or Beethoven composed music, or Shakespeare wrote poetry. He should sweep streets so well that all the hosts of heaven and earth will pause to say, here lived a great street sweeper who did his job well."

One of the things I most respect about my husband, David, is his work ethic. He's not only brilliant, good-looking and well read, he is every employer's dream working with integrity, tirelessly finishing a job to perfection even if it means staying at it well past five o'clock.

Straight out of college David started a job where he was over qualified and underpaid. Since jobs for new graduates with no professional work experience were hard to come by, he took it. Honestly, I thought he was crazy since someone in the 9th grade could have handled it. He said even though it wasn't his ultimate choice, it was a good place to start. As the weeks passed he was quickly given more and more responsibility. A few years later he went on to establish his own company. I don't think it ever crossed his mind that his first job was beneath him. I'm so glad he didn't listen to me.

Glen Baxley is one of the hardest working people I know. He's kind of a cowboy entrepreneur. Glen has several different businesses and jobs titles. One is to help farmers move their cattle from one location to another. Glen's partner in the cow herding business is his Catahoula Cur dog, Jake. The Catahoula breed originated in Catahoula, Louisiana. They were bred as working dogs and they're also hunters. President Teddy Roosevelt used Catahoulas for hunting and in 1979 Governor Edwin Edwards signed a bill and crowned the Cur as the official state dog of Louisiana.

This infamous dog had to work hard to earn and keep its place in society. How he worked determined whether or not he was honored to be part of the family or not. A dog at the turn of the twentieth century had to deliver above and beyond to cover the cost of his feed. In other words, there were no free rides.

One day after herding cattle Glen and Jake got in the flat bed work truck and headed for home. The ranch where they had been working that day was an hour and a half from home. Jake, as usual, was in the back of the truck, right behind the cab enjoying his ears flapping in the wind. About halfway home Glen noticed a group of deer on the side of the highway. Jake, seeing all the animals to round up, jumped off of the flat bed truck to chase them down. Glen pulled over to the shoulder of the road, flung open the door and started calling for Jake. After an hour of searching there were no deer and there was no Jake. He couldn't find his beloved business partner anywhere and since he was going 60 when Jake bailed out, Glen had little hope for his survival. He sadly got back in the truck and drove the 35 miles home. When he pulled into the driveway he put the truck in park and sat for a while still not believing what had happened.

Four days passed and Glen began to realize just how much he depended on Jake. The workload seemed double what it was before his disappearance. Just as that thought crossed his mind he looked up and saw what he thought was a deer walking down the road in the distance. His first concern was that one of his neighbors would hit the deer and seriously damage his truck. As the deer got closer, Glen realized that it wasn't a deer at all but his crazy dog, Jake. Glen was in shock. How did Jake survive that leap off the truck at 60 miles an hour? How did he make it through the concrete Springfield metroplex of 300,000 people, highways, and shopping malls? More importantly how did that dog sniff his way 35 miles back to his rural home?

Glen stood stunned as he watched a slobbery, wet, tail-wagging Jake jog into the driveway. Without even a pause this dedicated dog trotted right up to the truck, jumped in the back, and looked at Glen as to say, "Sorry I missed the last couple of days boss. I'm ready to go to work now."

Amazing! That is commitment to doing what it takes to get to where you want to go. We all need a little of Jake's passion in us.

Catahoulas already understand there aren't any free rides. We need to grasp that concept too. Oh, we might be able to squeak by for a while, but in the long haul, if we want something out of life, we need to get up and go to work. Make a plan and get started. Pray for guidance, strength and perseverance then put it in gear and go forward.

• •

We all need a little of Jake's passion in us.

• •

Like my friend Spike, I think Jake the dog lives by a creed too; work hard, take some risks, don't be afraid to get dirty, and never give up.

Chapter 2

Allow Some Margin In Your Life

"The trouble with the rat race is that even if you win, you're still a rat."

-Lily Tomlin

O f all the classes in four years of college, Biology lab was of my favorite. Three good friends were in the class too, meeting the most important requirement to be labeled worthwhile. As a bonus, the graduate student/lab instructor looked like one of the Greek god statues in the campus amphitheater. Perfect attendance was a given for all the girls. Dad definitely got his money's worth out of the tuition check that semester.

I arrived for lab one day to find a live frog on everyone's table. Since we were always taking apart dead things, this was a surprise. The lab instructions read: 1. Take your pan, fill it half full with room temperature water and put the frog in the pan. Check. 2. Place the pan on your Bunsen burner and turn it on low. Check?? 3. Every fifteen minutes during the next two hours gradually increase the temperature until just before the water boils, then remove the pan from the heat. Wait a minute! P.E.T.A hadn't even been founded yet, but I was ready to call someone! The too-cute-to-be-true lab instructor suddenly resembled Dr. Frankenstein. What was he trying to prove?

Over the next two hours we all watched, mesmerized as none of the frogs jumped out of the pans as the temperature inched up. No innocent frogs were killed. We rescued them all before it was too late.

This unusual lesson was about adaptability. The temperature change was so gradual the frogs didn't notice. They were in danger of boiling to death, but didn't jump out. The now-again-charming lab instructor's point was this: being adaptable is a good thing, but being adaptable to the point of danger and even death isn't.

That college experiment taught me more about people than frogs. Clearly, we are much smarter than frogs, but so much of the time we don't act like it. I watched a friend graduate from college and land an impressive job. She quickly learned the stress of college was nothing compared to that of the real world. She bought a condo and a puppy, volunteered for the church food pantry, and met Mr. Wonderful. Soon she was promoted at work and Mr. Wonderful proposed. Planning a wedding was supposed to be a dream, but it only gave her stomach cramps and headaches. She now had a job, a condo, a puppy, a food pantry, a wedding to plan and a fiancée who was feeling left out. Obviously it took more than two hours for the temperature to reach the boiling point for her but, like the frog, she hadn't noticed the gradual change, so she didn't know to jump out and say no to a few things.

• •

Clearly, we are much smarter than frogs, but so much of the time we don't act like it.

• •

My overly committed friend's body tried to get her attention through her belly and her head, but she ignored the pain and pushed on. My Uncle Arlo ignored his car's back-up warning beeper that sounded off every time he pulled out of his carport. The high tech sensory system detected the rise in the yard as something behind the car, so he paid no attention to the sound. That worked until one day the beeping was not about the lawn. My car was sitting in the driveway. My friend was ignoring her internal warning and she, too, was about to crash. She had gotten so used to feeling her stomach pain she disregarded it. It took a trip to the emergency room for her to finally realize the destruction course she was on. She eventually cut back on her workload and gave up some of her volunteer positions.

We're all at fault for overloading ourselves on some level. Somewhere along the way we forget how to say no. We need to learn our limits and figure out how to live within those limits without feeling guilty. We need to set our priorities and if someone questions them we should explain our priorities are just that, our own personal priorities. It was so freeing when I finally remembered what I learned in high school English class; "No" is a complete sentence. So, no explanation is necessary. Why do we have a need to explain everything? Is it a justification so we won't feel the sting of guilt for drawing some boundaries?

. . . .

We need to learn our limits and figure out how to live within those limits without feeling guilty

. . . .

In Galatians Paul writes about the fruit of the spirit; *love, joy, peace, patience, kindness, goodness, faithfulness, gentleness and self-control.* Nowhere is busyness mentioned, but in all our confusion we have come to equate busyness with godliness. That's so wrong on so many levels! Probably because we take on so much activity in the name of ministry we feel like it's an unwritten requirement. Stress and burnout are not respecters of the church or ministry of any kind. Everyone can fall into the busyness trap. "Oh, if I don't bake the cookies for the new members reception what will all the other women say about me," you think out loud.

Guess what? They're probably going to talk whether you bake cookies or not. So give it up. Sure we need to serve, but decide what you can handle without a prescription for heavy medication. Stop worrying about what everyone else is doing or not doing. Each of us is different and can manage different loads. Remember, we're no good to anyone if we're sick and exhausted.

Ecclesiastes 3:1 says *"There is a time for everything and a season for every activity under heaven."* Verses two through eight follow up with the list. The way I understand this is I can have it all and do it all but just not all at once. We have to learn to set some margin or buffer zone in our lives. Where did we get the idea it's a sign of weakness to take time out to rest and to take care of ourselves? Every time I get on a plane I am reassured it's not a weakness, it is a requirement. During the safety instructions the flight attendant says, "In the unlikely event we lose cabin pressure an oxygen mask will drop from the ceiling. Please place the mask on yourself first then help others around you."

Obviously, if you can't breathe you can't be helpful. Why do we spend the better part of our lives gasping for air when we really just need to step aside, sit down and take a deep breath?

Where is the margin in your life? Do you even know when you are coming close to the edge? Your margin probably doesn't look like anyone else's. Even though we're all different, there are a few suggestions that might keep you from falling off regardless how wide or narrow your boundaries are.

First, we need to set priorities and limits. What's important and required and what is optional? It's always clearer for me when I write things down. Look at the list and be brutally honest with yourself. Of those so-called requirements, what could really be considered an option? Now weed those things out of your list of must-dos. When you take it apart you'll find out how much you do because you think it is mandatory and expected when it's not.

Next, if you've forgotten, re-learn how to say no. For some of us, saying no, is just not easy. We finally had to establish a family rule stating Jim was not allowed to answer the doorbell because it was so hard for him to say no, especially to the Girl Scouts and their cookies. You don't have to be rude, but smile when asked to do things you know you can't handle, and say something like, "I am going to let you take care of that this time" or "That's just not going to work for me tomorrow."

Once you do it a few times you'll realize the people asking will find someone else to do the job if you can't. You might even want to make an unwritten rule for yourself limiting the extras in your life to two or three or whatever you feel is manageable. If you know you are maxed out in the extras category you don't have to even think when asked to add to it. No is your automatic answer. Not right now, but maybe some time in the future.

Most importantly, you need quiet time every day. Reading, prayer, and meditation will keep you farther away from the falling off point. You may have several small kids and the only scripture you read some days is in a bedtime Bible story. That's OK. Remember you're in a season of life. They'll grow up. You can even pray while driving the car. Just don't bow your head. Believe it or not God hears you with your eyes open. The most important thing is to acknowledge Him and know He is your strength. Take a few minutes, find a quiet spot and just be still.

We set up a blue plastic kiddy pool in Jill's bedroom when our dog Sally's due date was near. Instinctively she knew to give birth there. That was her little family home until the pups opened their eyes and could climb out. On days when Sally grew weary of being a mother and had had enough of her babies climbing all over her, she would get out of the blue pool, retreat to another room and stretch out in the sun for a while. She needed a break to regroup and rest. It was like she knew a break would help her be a better mom.

When I was at home with three small very active kids, I would sometimes hide in my closet. Like Sally, I knew I needed a time out. I love Snickers candy bars and kept a stash in the closet under my sweatshirts. On days when I was creeping toward the edge I would retreat to my closet for a quiet moment and some chocolate. I would pray... "God thank you for the candy bar I am about to receive. Thank you for these precious children even though they are driving me totally crazy. Father, I do understand why some mammals eat their young! Please give me strength to be a good mother. In Jesus name, Amen!" Meanwhile I could hear the kids. "Mom. Mom. MOM!" "Where did she go?" "I don't know." "Where is she?"

As brief as it was, the tiny retreat pulled me back to center. In Matthew 11:28 Jesus said, *"Come to me, all you who are weary and burdened, and I will give you rest.* The come to me part is the key. We have to take the time to step away and go to Him.

• •

As brief as it was, the tiny retreat pulled me back to center.

• •

To keep some balance we also need to set some mental margin for ourselves. There is a fine line between concern and full-blown, hand wringing worry. Yes, we need to be concerned, but where does worry take us. In reality a high percentage of what we are consumed with worry over never happens. What a waste of time and energy!

As a United States congressman, one of the ways Roy Blunt keeps in touch with the citizens of his district is by town meetings set up via phone. The first time I answered one of these phone calls I almost hung up thinking it was yet another political fundraiser. I'm so glad I didn't. The call from a computer told me I would shortly be connected with a meeting already in session. Then the feed went live to Congressman Blunt answering call-in questions from southwest Missourians. It was fascinating and what I learned reshaped some of the ways I think not just about politics, but life. The congressman fielded questions about everything from the shaky Social Security system and the rising cost of oil to the future of the local farmer and the uncertainty of pork belly prices. Pork bellies? What is that about?

Of all the questions, the one from Margaret, who lived in a tiny rural community, intrigued me the most. "Congressman Blunt, I was sitting here having some diner with Frank when your town meeting call came. Thank you for staying in touch with us and listening to our concerns."

"You are quite welcome, Margaret. It's actually part of my job to stay connected with you from Washington," Mr. Blunt answered. "What's on your mind tonight?"

"Well sir, I'm wondering, should we be more worried about the terrorists or the bird flu," she questioned.

He laughed then continued to give a very comforting, politically correct answer about our extremely efficient Center for Disease Control and the steadfastness of the United States' war on terror. I smiled and wished he had answered with something like, "Well, Margaret, why don't you worry about terrorists on Monday, Wednesday, and Friday and then cover the Bird Flu on Tuesday, Thursday and Saturday. Take Sunday off and give it a rest." However, that type of response might have lessened his chances for another term in office.

We might not call in to a town hall meeting like Margaret, but all of us have concerns and questions that keep us awake at night. So much of it is nothing we have any control over. Different types of temperaments handle worry from one extreme to the other. Some worry all the time, others don't worry ever. If I let myself, I could fall into the worry-all-the-time category. I had to make a decision to give a lot of it up. I was too afraid I might end up being an old, crazy cat lady walking around in my robe and a shower cap all day. The term worried sick is real.

Stress and worry cause or aggravate the majority of all the illnesses and diseases we deal with today.

• •

Stress and worry cause or aggravate the majority of all the illnesses and diseases we deal with today.

• •

Philippians 4:6 reminds me God has it covered. *"Do not be anxious for anything, but in everything, by prayer and supplication, present your requests to God."* He's in charge and reveals information to me on a need to know basis. That way I can handle one day at a time. I had to put down the what if worry. It is smart to prepare, but it does no good to worry ahead. Do you ever see dogs worry? Well, maybe Chihuahuas do. I think other dogs most likely feel Chihuahuas need medical help for their tension and stress.

On my computer when I push print sometimes a little note pops up saying, "If you choose to continue, you will print outside the margin. Do you want to continue?" It's a helpful reminder. I get to make a choice about how I want my finished product to look. We all get reminders everyday that our lives are squeezing out the margin. Don't ignore the indicator lights.

Learn to leave some margin in your life. You'll miss out on a lot if you don't. So much of the good stuff happens in the margin.

Chapter 3

Is It Really Worth It?

"A bulldog can whip a skunk, but some things just aren't worth it."

-Unknown

W hen Stephanie and Liz faced each other, it was as if they were looking in a mirror. They were as identical as twins could be. With silky auburn hair, ivory skin and turquoise blue eyes they could silence a room just by walking in. They were seldom apart, so after high school graduation the decision to attend different colleges hundreds of miles apart stunned their family and friends. After the shock subsided, everyone agreed it would be good for the girls to discover who they were individually as they transitioned into young adults. Besides, with technology they were truly only a text or call away from each other.

In late summer, after tearful goodbyes, Liz and Stephanie headed off to their respective colleges entering a whole new world of life experiences. They were in touch with each other several times a day the first two weeks, but as their individual schedules accelerated into high gear, the calls, texts and emails drifted further and further apart. They both were absorbed into college life on their own.

In mid-December focusing to study for finals was more of a challenge than the exams themselves. The girls felt like six-year- olds again as Christmas break crept closer and closer. Stephanie got home first so a full family greeting committee was at the airport when Liz landed. Stephanie was not prepared for what she saw when her sister walked through the security gates. In fact she didn't realize it was Liz until she was almost taken to the ground in a bear hug.

"Liz?" Stephanie screamed as she held her sister at arm's length.

Her brain couldn't process fast enough. Liz had cropped her long copper tresses into a pixie cut and she was now blonde. To make matters worse, while Stephanie was gaining the freshman fifteen, Liz had earned a position on her college cross-country track team and had lost ten pounds.

"Oh my gosh! What have you done to yourself," Stephanie squeaked like Mini Mouse on helium.

"Wild, huh?" Liz beamed. Some friends encouraged me to try out for the track team and I discovered I love running and I'm actually pretty good. I'm in the best shape ever. My hair took so much time after I joined the team I just had to cut it. And I've always wondered what I would look like as a blonde, so I gave it a try. Well, what do you think?

Stephanie stood frozen for a few seconds then realized she had to respond. Her determination to stay calm vaporized the minute she opened her mouth.

• •

Her determination to stay calm vaporized the minute she opened her mouth.

• •

"What do I think?" she started. "I think you are the most selfish, self centered person on the planet. How could you? You never even asked me! I thought it was important to you that we looked alike. Now no one would suspect we are even related. I knew deep down it was a bad idea for you to go to that liberal east-coast college! What have you turned in to? Aaaah!!

Wisely, Liz headed to the baggage claim area without saying a word. Stephanie's anger blasted even higher when she found out the rest of the family was in on the surprise. She felt absolutely betrayed by everyone and deep inside she was jealous of Liz's bravery to make a change and jealous she looked so good. She refused to talk to her sister for two days and then when she did start speaking it was only when necessary. Christmas was definitely a memory-maker, just not the one the family had thought it would be.

Liz decided to go back to campus a full two weeks earlier than planned just to escape the turmoil. How could her twin turn on her? She went on a trip with the track team during spring break that year and found a job in her college community for the summer. Over the next three years she only made the trip back home for Christmas. The relationship with her sister, once so precious, had crumbled to ruin and over the next few years they rarely spoke. When they did talk, the conversation usually turned in to an argument. It was heartbreaking for the entire family.

31

About six months before the girls' ten-year high school reunion, Stephanie received a call from the class president, a friend she hadn't seen for years. She explained all the plans for the upcoming reunion and in conversation asked Stephanie how Liz was doing.

"Oh, I don't know. Fine I guess. We hardly ever talk and I only see her at Christmas," Stephanie answered slowly.

"You're kidding me!" her shocked friend said. "You two were so close in high school.... like best friends as well as sisters. Something really bad must have happened to unravel such a tight relationship. What was it?"

Stephanie sat quietly with the phone on her ear thinking about what her friend had asked.

"Now that you bring it up, I really can't remember what exactly started it," Stephanie answered, wondering what had actually happened.

As the conversation ended and she hung up the phone it dawned on her she had no idea why she and Liz had slowly drifted apart. She just knew she was mad.

As sad as that situation is, it's all too common... relationships in ruin because of a pointless disagreement that dragged on so long no one remembers how it got started. We all can think of an example or may have actually suffered such a casualty. George Patton, the famous United States Army general, once said, "Never go into battle unless you have something to gain by winning." This is a powerful quote. In other words, don't put on your helmet and yell *Charge!* unless it is serious. Choose your battles and choose them wisely. The longer I live and the more people I meet, the more I realize how important this concept is. Life is much too short for unnecessary battles. They heap on stress, wear us out and for what?

• •

*George Patton, the famous United States Army general,
once said, "Never go into battle unless you have something
to gain by winning."*

• •

While raising three kids, there was always potential for battle lines to be drawn. Jim and I asked ourselves three questions before we took action: Is it illegal? Is it immoral? Is it dangerous? If the answer was no to each of those questions, we usually chose not to go in to battle. Kids, especially teens, have to be told no so many times. Choose carefully what's battle worthy. Decide before an issue comes up if you are willing to go to the front lines. It keeps you from being caught off-guard and reduces unnecessary clashes.

Many times, knowingly or not, we pick fights. If your husband is driving to the grocery store and takes a different route than you normally do, why do you feel it necessary to point out that his route is actually a quarter mile longer than the route you take? This is dangerous because it can swing wide-open the door to old arguments and reopen battle wounds. When that happens, pent up feeling come tumbling out without warning. A simple statement challenging judgment on something so insignificant can be taken as a declaration of war. So what if your route is shorter! Shut your mouth and enjoy the ride. We really should put our big kid pants on and get over the need to be right about really silly, pointless stuff. We all know those, like a self-appointed high school hall monitor, who demand explanation or proof about trivial things. I try to ignore their constant jabs, because I can end up in a duel with them. *Proverbs 17:14 says: "Starting a quarrel is like breaching a dam; so drop the matter before a dispute breaks out".*

Many painful situations can be diffused if we ask ourselves a few simple things instead of marching on. Before questioning someone or sharing information, I have found that it is best to slow down and not respond to my first impulse blurting out advice or opinions. If Stephanie had responded differently to Liz's new look, I wonder how those ten years of relationship wasteland might have been lived out differently. Many times things will work out without saying a word.

Ask yourself, "On a scale of 1-10 how important is this?" Will it matter in two days, two weeks or two years? Like the illegal, immoral, dangerous check list we used, you, too, might want to have some questions as a determining filter before you respond.

Before you open your mouth, you need to consider if what you are about to say is worth risking a relationship. A friend and I made a promise when our kids were very young. As they grew up we agreed we would share things with each other even though it could be painful and disappointing. That was easy to commit to when the kids were in kindergarten. I had to weigh the possible consequences when I stuck to my promise and went to my friend during their high school years. Thankfully, I was met with an open heart and listening ear. We are still close friends today. Unfortunately, not all confrontations have such a positive ending. Calculate your willingness to take a loss.

• •

Before you open your mouth, you need to consider if what you are about to say is worth risking a relationship.

• •

Romans 12:18 clearly says, "If it is possible, as far as it depends on you, live at peace with everyone." Peace is our ultimate goal, even though we live in the real world of constant craziness and turmoil. If you do find yourself looking into the face of conflict, here are some guidelines for the "as far as it depends on you" part of that scripture. Remember, you really are the only person you have control of.

First, fight your natural response and *don't become defensive.* Why do we act as if our honor has totally been violated when someone else sees a situation differently than we do? Former Arkansas Governor Mike Huckabee's response to a media question when he was vying for the presidential nomination is one I'll always remember. When asked about being conservative, he responded, "I may be conservative, but I'm not angry." Now, that is classic. *"A fool shows his annoyance at once, but a prudent man overlooks an insult"* is what Proverbs instructs. We can disagree, but we don't have to become defensive or down right aggressive. Always remember, someone else's opinion is likely as strong as yours.

Secondly, *control your temper.* Because your dad has a short fuse is no excuse for you. Being hot tempered is not a genetic handicap. Angry Stephanie can't blame losing her temper on her coppery red hair. It's not about genes or hair color; it's about making the wise choice to control your temper. We've all heard people say, " I just blow up, clear the air, and then it's over", like that's an OK thing to do. A bomb also blows up, the air clears, it's over and 911 is called in to rescue the wounded and repair the damage. The fall-out from a blow-up is always toxic.

• •

Being hot tempered is not a genetic handicap.

• •

Next, *use kind words.* Put everything on yourself by saying things like "I feel…, How I see it…, I think I'm right, but I could be wrong." Avoid spouting off things you'll be so sorry for once you calm down. Also, increased volume doesn't produce better results. Why do we tend to shout when the person we are in conflict with is usually right in front of us? Pointing at the other person and make accusations is not useful. If you do, more than likely, the person you are wagging your finger at will become defensive and then you're off to the races. *Proverbs 18:2 explains, "A gentle answer turns away wrath, but a harsh word stirs up anger."* Simply put, be kind.

When things start to heat up, *listen carefully,* you many learn something. We are so focused on making sure our feelings and our point of view are heard that we forget to listen to what the other person is trying to say. Most arguments are started over a misunderstanding. We make assumptions based on what we think or believe to be true when most of the time, we don't have the facts. In the book of James we are told to *"Be quick to listen, slow to speak, and slow to anger."* A large number of fights could totally be avoided if we would just listen. Jill addresses the art of listening later on. Understanding how to listen is crucial for all relationships.

Finally, be humble enough to admit your mistakes, ask forgiveness then get over it. Granted, some things will never be totally resolved. It would be nice if they all were, but that's not reality. All you can do is your part in the pursuit of living in peace. Call a truce and lay down your weapons.

To me, the saddest battles are those within a family. The conflict between Liz and Stephanie is a painful illustration. Stephanie advanced, Liz retreated and the rest of the family had no idea what to do. If we could only realize we are on the same team. We're not only on the same team; we're fighting the same battles. Why do we end up fighting each other? It would be like an army turning on it's self. Instead of watching the backs of comrades, an internal revolution breaks out. It's hard to tell who's a friend and who's a foe. Families can learn from schools of fish…. they stick together, they swim in the same direction and they avoid collisions. In Ephesians 6:12 we are reminded whom the real enemy is and that we are in the battle together. *"For our struggle is not against flesh and blood, but against the rulers, against the authorities, against the powers of this dark world and against the spiritual forces of evil in the heavenly realm."*

Warfare is hard work whether it is physical, mental, emotional, or spiritual and leaves you drained and often wounded. So much fighting is energy wasted and conflicts often end with friendships and relationships destroyed. I challenge you to be wise in what you choose to battle over and whom you choose to battle with. If you do find yourself at war, remember some of the suggested battle strategies.

• •

Warfare is hard work whether it is physical, mental, emotional, or spiritual and leaves you drained and often wounded.

• •

A bulldog probably can whip a skunk, but why bother. The bragging rights just aren't worth the consequences. Dogs usually tangle with a skunk one time and afterwards learn to avoid them. We should be so wise. Weigh the costs, choose the battle very carefully, and make sure it is about something you are willing to take a bullet for.

37

Chapter 4

You Don't Have To Have A Lot Of Money To Have A Lot Of Class

"Class is an aura of confidence that is being sure without being cocky. Class has nothing to do with money."

-Ann Landers

When I think of classy people what flashes across my mind is a picture of Audrey Hepburn in a little black dress sitting ladylike at a dinner party across from a handsome man in a bow tie sipping champagne. They are discussing Shakespeare, the opera and talking about their latest travels to Paris. I've always been intrigued by these people. I've met a few in real life. They are educated, well read, well groomed, and very well spoken.

When I was invited to a dinner with a group of Los Angeles businesswomen, I was honored by the invitation and quickly accepted. Knowing this was going to be quite an affair, I arrived that evening in my own little classic black dress. After being seated, it didn't take long to realize I was probably at the table with five of the most educated women in the city. Three of them were doctors, each in

39

specialized fields, and the other two were respected attorneys. All had graduated with honors from Ivy League schools. The conversation was stimulating and motivating and I left the restaurant energized and ready to take on the world. As I drove home thinking about dinner, what struck me was this - these women were not classy because of their impressive diplomas, hefty incomes, or stunning beauty. Their purpose in life was not to just look good and make money, but more importantly to make a difference. That's what set them apart. They cared about so much more than just themselves. They had class.

In the middle of all the chaos planning our wedding, Mom gave David and me a full day course with June Moore, one of the top business and social etiquette teachers in the country. David balked a little, but secretly got a kick out of his soon to be southern debutant mother-in-law giving him a manners course as a gift. Since David, at that time, was serving an internship at the capital in Washington, DC, I'm sure Mom felt what he could learn from Mrs. Moore would serve him well then and in the future.

On the day of our class, as we got closer to Little Rock, I could tell David was having second thoughts about spending a day with the manners lady. I think we were both picturing a woman with a tight bun on top of her head and board straight posture. She would probably be holding a ruler to use if necessary and she would most likely pull on our ears for any sudden wrong move. When we turned into her driveway, to our surprise, she came outside to greet us. To our relief, June Moore was warm and kind and southern as sweet tea. Our nightmare images disappeared and we immediately relaxed.

She invited us in and, of course, had cookies and lemonade waiting. Before we started the first lesson, she made clear the purpose of manners. "Manners," she passionately explained, "are not about YOU. Manners are about honoring those you are with."

What we learned that day is probably some of the most valuable information we could have ever received. It will help us wherever we go. We learned everything from how to introduce people and handle awkward social situations to the best way to be a courteous guest and what it took to be a gracious host. We finished the day in a beautiful restaurant where we, not only enjoyed an incredible meal, but were also guided through appropriate dinner protocol. That night we drove back home with our image of manners being stuffy and snooty totally changed as we had discovered that etiquette was all about honoring others.

I don't think it's a natural part of our character...honoring others. We are basically selfish, automatically considering ourselves before anyone else. It's almost like a defense mechanism we use so we're assured we won't be left out. I guess that's the reason we all rush to the front of a serving line at a party like we haven't eaten in days. I don't know about you, but most of the people I know haven't missed a meal lately. If they have, it was on purpose.

Have you ever noticed courtesy has a weird sort of a ripple effect? It must be part of our twisted human nature. If you are polite by stepping back and allowing someone with fewer items to go ahead of you at the checkout or if you let a person in a line of traffic, others will start to do the same. I honestly think it's because no one wants to be outdone, even in being kind and honorable.

• •

Have you ever noticed courtesy has a weird sort of a ripple effect?

• •

We can find a perfect example of how to honor others by examining the life of Jesus. Personally, I think he was the classiest man ever to walk the face of this earth. At the Passover meal he not only honored his disciples by waiting for them to be seated before he began, but he also picked up a towel and washed their feet. It was customary in those days to wash your feet before a meal. It was most likely because diners actually reclined on an elbow to eat and the odor from the feet next to you might totally ruin your dinner.

Everyone wore sandals and miles were walked everyday. The desert was dry and I'm sure feet cracked and bled from the long journeys. I'm sure Jesus bathed some really nasty feet. He did it to show the disciples what real honor and service looked like. In John 13:14-15 Jesus said, *"Now that I your Lord and Teacher have washed your feet, you should wash one another's feet. I have set you an example that you should do as I have done for you."* He gave us a perfect picture of what serving looks like. Now I don't necessarily think we are to wash feet, but we are to serve one another with a posture of honor and appreciation. Simple things make a big difference.

• •

Simple things make a big difference.

• •

My friend, Kay, volunteers and serves for several charity organizations in the Los Angeles area. The Humane Society is her favorite. One of the fundraisers she has pioneered is the *Take Your Dog Shopping* event. It is held annually at a very upscale department store before regular shopping hours.

Hors d'oeuvres are served for the dog owners and special water dishes and treats are readily available for the pooches. A pet photographer is on site for take home souvenirs. Hundreds of dollars of door prizes are given away and thousands are donated to the Human Society. A percentage of sales from the host store goes to the charity so there is a literal shopping frenzy.

The first time my dog Bro and I attended I was stunned and think Bro felt like David did on the trip to Little Rock, nervous. Over 200 dogs and their owners were there and all were behaving as if they had attended Mrs. Moore's manners class, the humans and the dogs. There were poodles, Scotties, sheep dogs, Afghans, mixed breeds of all kinds, every little purse dog imaginable and even a pit bull or two. Some of the dogs had on clothes and jewelry that cost more than what I was wearing!

I even watched a very preppy dressed man in front of a designer dog bowl display ask his three standard poodles which bowl they would like to have. As he put one bowl behind his back and held one out in front of them he said, "Girls, would you like this one" then switching bowls," or this one?" When he couldn't read their answer he said smiling, "Oh, let's just get them both."

Unbelievable!

In a situation that could have been total chaos, the worst thing that happened was a puddle or two left by overly excited attendees. This was a situation where there was a lot of money and a lot of class. However, the dogs were not impressed at all. They were just enjoying the big party and each other. The classiest thing that went on that day was Kay raised a nice sum for a very worth cause. She was certainly focused on serving others.

I was in an exclusive boutique type store in Beverly Hills a few years ago. It was one of those stores I only walk in when I see that red SALE sign in the window. The clothing and accessories were very beautiful and very expensive, but the red sign was in the window so I went in. A sharply dressed, perfectly groomed, man introduced himself as Anthony and I in turn introduced myself. In addition to all the sale items I took to the dressing room he brought me some lovely regular priced items just for fun. He checked on me periodically. "Ms. Jones, how are you doing? Ms. Jones, can I get anything for you? Ms. Jones, would you like some ice water or iced tea?" I knew I was in a truly classy place because the bottom line was all about service.

• •

I knew I was in a truly classy place because the bottom line was all about service.

• •

Not long after Anthony brought a glass of tea complete with a fresh sprig of mint, there was quite a ruckus in the dressing room hallway. An older, obviously well to do, woman who sounded like Queen Elizabeth evidently had run into a friend. "Oh, hellooooo dahling! Ohhh, it's so divine to see you! I missed you in Paris last month. Oh, I don't blame

44

you for staying home with your husband. You better be careful with him. He is quite the good looker. Hummmm."

Before I opened my dressing room door to see what was going on, I thought the movie character Mrs. Doubtfire was in the store. "Tah Tah," she quipped swishing her hand in the air as she hurried by me headed to pay for her armload of clothes.

About that time, Anthony was walking down the hall to check on me. As the Queen Elizabeth sounding lady brushed by totally ignoring him, he smiled at me and rolled his eyes.

"Wow, Anthony, she must be one of your more important customers!" I said, wondering what her grand total was going to be at the cash register. Anthony simply said with a grin, "Ms. Jones, people are people."

• •

"Ms. Jones, people are people."

• •

Anthony was so right and I try to remember that phrase when I find myself in a situation when others clearly feel they are above everyone else.

The pit bull by definition is one of the most dangerous breeds of dogs. Supposedly they consider themselves better than anyone else and you better not mess with them. I always think of them as big bowed up cocky guys named Brutus or Chuck with tattoos all over their bodies, shaved heads, behind bars doing hard time. What was interesting at the doggy shopping event was watching the pit bull and the poodle socialize. They would politely sniff one another, as to say, "Hey there, great party, huh?" Seeing these polar opposites get along makes me think we humans have something to learn. They knew like Anthony knew, dogs are dogs.

Cesar Millan is a brilliant dog trainer, best known from National Geographic's *The Dog Whisper*. His technique of introducing dogs by taking them on a walk side-by-side intrigues me. I think his main purpose is for them to meet each other as equals. It's like forced humility and levels the playing field.

Bro and I would take long walks every day in our neighborhood. It was good for both of us. I even considered buying him a tee shirt to wear on our walks that has "Personal Trainer" printed on the back. We'd pass dog friends and their owners every few blocks. Sometimes the dogs would sniff and move on. Once I was tempted to sniff another dog owner for fun, but decided that was just too big of a risk.

Every once in a while when Bro would meet another dog face to face I sensed tension between the two as they sized each other up. Who is the strongest, who is the smartest, who is the best looking? Eventually one would humble himself and walk away. The one with the most class, who knows a dogfight would solve nothing, usually turned and headed on down the sidewalk. I think that's why it's best we walk along side of each other instead of facing off. We just get along better.

Women really have to be careful about meeting face to face, too. The next time you're introduced to a new person be aware of your initial thoughts. Do you try to categorize her? What breed does she come from? What does her pedigree look like? When was the last time she was groomed? How snobbish and uppity is that? When women act that way, more than likely, that's why they're compared to a female dog.

Cesar points out in his book, *Cesar's Way,* dogs naturally migrate in packs. The pack he works with is like one big team of all breeds headed in the same direction. Why can't we do that; all breeds, all races, all people together on a great migrate. We're on this expedition together. You are not more important than anyone else - your job, your family, your education, your race, your wealth. The world may argue with it, but that's simply fact in God's economy.

Martin Luther King, Jr. said it flawlessly. "I have a dream that my four little children will, one day, live in a nation where they will not be judged by the color of their skin but by the content of their character..."

What kind of reputation are you building? How are you honoring others? Who are you serving? What difference are you making? Honor, humility, serving and making a difference... That's real class and it doesn't cost a cent.

• •

What kind of reputation are you building?

• •

Chapter 5

Did You Hear That?

"He who answers before listening-that is his folly and his shame."

-Proverbs 18:13

I sometimes wonder if I should have been born to parents who worked in a circus or a zoo. Animals are my friends. All of them, but the under-dogs are by far my favorite. Left to my own vices by the age of five I would have opened a homeless shelter for strays. I guess I actually did but it was a make shift system that my family tolerated. At one point we had an orphaned fawn that I bottle fed, a raccoon who was fascinated with my white blonde hair and a cat my brothers kept trying to get rid of with a BB gun and bottle rockets. My whole family was totally unaware of the fact I had put a baby bassinet under the porch and every morning after breakfast I would sneak out and put down a bowl of milk out for the terrorized stray. No one could imagine why that cat kept coming back for more of what the boys were dishing out.

One morning Dad caught me barefoot in my PJs on the front porch with the milk. He just smiled and went back inside without saying a

49

word. Later that day he announced to my brothers that he was officially calling for a cease-fire on shooting at the weird looking stray cat. The next week she became an official pet after a trip to the vet for necessary shots and so forth. One hundred dollars later I had a cat named Peanut Butter and Jelly, but we called her Kitty for short. Kitty the cat, Coco the raccoon, and Sugar the fawn all became best friends with our black Labrador retriever, Josie.

• •

One hundred dollars later I had a cat named Peanut Butter and Jelly, but we called her Kitty for short.

• •

Josie was my constant companion. Being the third kid in a very active family had its advantages but there was one big down side; everyone was always busy. Sometimes the only one who wasn't busy was Josie. She was always on call. We took walks, we played Barbie, and we played dress up. I was always amazed that my dresses would fit her. She looked like a four-legged ballerina as we proudly danced around the house in our costumes giving, whoever would watch, a fashion show.

Josie was very popular with the boy dogs in the neighborhood and over five years became the mother to three litters of puppies. Jake and Pro were two of her Labrador boyfriends who lived down the road. So many of our neighbors were Labrador owners that I didn't think you were normal unless you had a Lab or two.

I spent a lot of hot summer days throwing sticks into the lake for Josie, Pro, and Jake. After I had run off all of their energy, I would line them up in a row on the cool grass. It was amazing how well they would listen to a five year old. I think being the youngest, I never got to boss anyone around so that was my only chance. I would take my favorite Dr. Seuss book out of my bag and open the cover, smooth out the page and begin reading. Th...Th...The Ca... Ca...Cat In The Ha...Ha...Hat. The dogs would sit politely and listen to me read as I sounded out every single word. It would take me, what felt like forever, to get through one book. I was a very s-l-o-w reader.

• •

I think being the youngest, I never got to boss anyone around so that was my only chance.

• •

My friend Lindsay, now a doctor specializing in hematology, was in my kindergarten class. She was such a good reader and I wanted to read like her. Lindsay never had to sound out any of her words, she always got to read the thick books and she never had the teacher breathing down her neck. Reading was so easy for her. My plan was to practice all summer so I could read the thick books when I got to first grade.

Something amazing happen by late August. I was reading thicker books and sounding out fewer words. I had moved from Dr. Seuss on to The Magic School Bus books. I think the dogs where glad for the variety. They listened so intently and rarely fell asleep. I not only felt understood, I gained confidence. Looking back to that summer, I realize I learned a lot about listening from my dog friends.

We all should value the art of listening. In our jazzed-up, faster-than-a-speeding-bullet world we would all benefit by slowing down and taking in what others are saying to us. Communication is far less about talking than it is about listening. That alone makes listening the foundation for strong relationships.

How many times have you heard people say, "You never listen to me!" or "Did you hear a word I said?" or "Hello, are you in there?" When statements like that are made, you can bet there are some hurt feelings. When your friends and family don't think you are paying attention to them, what you are saying without uttering a word is, "You're not important enough for me to listen." We would never intend to communicate that, but that's exactly what's being heard.

The simple fact is this; people are happier when they feel like they have been heard. If a teen-aged son wants to go somewhere you really don't think is a good idea, try listening to him make his request and letting him explain all the reasons he should be allowed to go. Don't respond just listen. Doing that, you are honoring him by showing respect for his feelings. And many times when kids explain requests out loud they will talk themselves out of what they first thought they wanted. It might be the first time they have actually listened to all the details themselves. There's no need for them to become defensive, because they are allowed to explain themselves without any pushback.

• •

The simple fact is this; people are happier when they feel like they have been heard.

• •

Different temperaments listen differently. A real sensitive, caring person will probably not only listen to every word you say, but can also be easily brought to tears just by hearing the details of a struggle you might be having. On the other hand you might feel as if you have to hold another person's face in your hands just to get eye contact with them. Personality is no excuse; we can all learn how to listen better. Some of us just have to work harder at it than others.

Women listen very differently than men. Research shows they actually tend to be better listeners. Women can process between 200 to 300 words a minute sometimes with gusts up to 400. You can only imagine how overwhelming it must be to a man. I actually believe that many times when I think David is not listening to me, he really is. The blank look on his face is just a by-product of his trying to process what I am saying.

The way women communicate can also confuse men. I don't know what it is, but women can clearly understand each other without completing sentences. My friend Rachelle, her husband Aaron, David and I were out to dinner one night when Rachelle said excitedly," Did you just see the thing that she had with the deal over there?" I said, "Yes! I really can't believe she didn't use the other one, but I really like it." Rachelle said, "Me too. I think that's just awesome."

• •

The way women communicate can also confuse men.

• •

Thoroughly confused and frustrated David said, "Stop! Hold on! Aaron and I have no idea what you two are talking about." I'm sure Rachelle and I both responded with that are-you-kidding-me look. We knew exactly what we were talking about, but the men were lost. The good thing was David knew to ask questions when he felt derailed in the conversation. We need to remember just because we know what we are saying doesn't mean who we are talking to understands. That puts some responsibility on the speaker to make sure the listener is tracking with him or her.

Since being a good listener is a learned trait for most of us, there are a few things we can consciously practice. Eye contact is really important. I'm sure you have tried to talk to someone who won't look you in the eye or even in the face. That is so distracting to me because not only do I try to follow their eyes to see what they are focusing on, I wonder the whole time if I am being heard. Concentrate on looking at the speaker as if you are hearing the most important information you can possibly be privileged to. Have the courtesy to not watch TV or text while you are in conversation. That's just rude and shows disrespect to the person talking. If you absolutely must tend to something, please excuse yourself then return as soon as possible.

• •

Concentrate on looking at the speaker as if you are hearing the most important information you can possibly be privileged to.

• •

Respond verbally and non verbally. Raised eyebrows and a head nod say a lot. Interject things like "And then what happened?" or "What did you do then?" It shows you are following what the person is saying. Empathize with, "Oh" or "Really?" or "Unbelievable" to show concern. This may sound silly and so trivial, but the results will surprise you.

Ask questions. People feel honored when you want to know what is going on in their life. I never really understood how important this is until late one afternoon at a large convention. Mom and I had been on our feet all day in several meetings so we decided to grab a cup of coffee at a Starbuck's kiosk. As we approached the counter, a very tired and disgruntled young woman peered up over her glasses with look of a dread. "Hi there," I said. "Is it too late to get a cup of coffee? We know it's only five minutes until you close, so we will take whatever you have left." The coffee girl nodded her head as she relaxed a little and forced a weak smile. "How was your day?" Mom innocently asked.

All of a sudden she threw her hands in the air and went into a monologue of anger and frustration. "I have been here since eight this morning all by myself. No one has come to relieve me. I finally just left a while ago to go to the ladies room and when I returned there were five totally put-off customers. I apologized and explained my situation, but they really didn't care. They were in a hurry and wanted their coffee! Then I ran out of ice and one man yelled at me and stormed off."

And on and on she went. All we did was focus on her, listen intently adding an occasional, "Wow", "No way", "Whoa!"

When she handed us our coffee, she said, " I am so sorry to just carry on like that. Thank you so much for listening. You have been so kind and I feel so much better. I think I'll go home, have some dinner and take a hot bath."

All in the world she needed was for someone to hear her out and show some understanding. It really doesn't take a lot to make a big difference in someone's day, just by listening. Ask questions. You may be surprised at what you will be told. We sure were.

When you are in conversation, don't interrupt. Let whoever is speaking finish a thought or story without butting in. Even though you might have something very important to say, hang on. In fact, if you are really listening you aren't focused on what you are going to say next. You are focused on what the person speaking has to say.

• •

When you are in a conversation, don't interrupt.

• •

Don't randomly try to change the subject. Just like interrupting, changing the subject is rude and shows a lack of interest in what your conversation partner is saying. It's as if you think you have something much more interesting to talk about. And, what ever you do, please be aware of the "one-upping" that we are all guilty of at some time. You know when it is coming when you hear yourself say, "You think that is bad" or "You'll never believe this…!" Stop yourself before you even get started. What does it prove? More importantly how does it make the other person feel?

The last thing to remember is, if you are talking you can't be learning. A farmer had a litter of seven AKC registered pups. When they were eight weeks old he was posting a hand painted "Pups For Sale" sign when a young boy in his overalls came walking up the road. "Excuse me, Mister. I would like to buy one of your dogs," he said, startling the farmer.

The farmer laughed as he patted the boy on the head and said, "Son, I doubt you have enough money to buy one of these. They are pure bred hunting dogs."

The little boy reached deep into the pocket of his overalls and pulled out twenty-nine cents. He held up the coins in the palm of his hand toward the farmer and said, "Will this be enough for me to a least have a look".

The farmer smiled and motioned the boy toward the barn. As they opened the creaky gate, all the excited pups came rushing out to greet them. Six of the puppies seemed to be in one group zipping around the yard, but the seventh was lagging behind. The boy pointed to the runt puppy that couldn't keep up with the rest of the litter.

"Oh Sir, I want that one!"

The farmer said, "Boy you don't want that one. You are young and that pup can't run and play and keep up with you like these other dogs can.

"Sir," the boy tried to continue. But the farmer interrupted saying, "That dog has some defects and he will never be as strong as the others."

"But, Mister," the boy again tried to continue but the insistent man interrupted him again.

"You don't know what you are saying son. I would be cheating you to sell that one to you for your twenty-nine cents," the farmer kept pushing and talking over the boy like an auctioneer. What did this kid know anyway?

Finally the boy stopped trying to get a word in and quietly lifted up his overalls revealing the brace on his leg. He simply said, "You see sir, I can't run and play and keep up with everyone, either. I just want a dog like me that understands. I think we could have a real good time together."

It's amazing what you might learn if you will just be quiet and listen. The Message translation of Proverbs 21:11 makes it so clear: *"Simpletons only learn the hard way, but the wise learn by listening."*

• •

It's amazing what you might learn if you will just be quiet and listen.

• •

God gave us two ears and one mouth for a reason. You and I should take inventory of our listening habits and make the needed changes. There is a big difference in hearing and really listening. Earnestly listening shows honor, places value on someone, and demonstrates how much we care. What a wonderful gift you can extend. However, you will be the one to benefit the most.

I learned as a little girl, dogs are great listeners. They hang on your every word, they don't interrupt, they cock their heads to listen more closely and they never change the subject. It's no wonder a dog is man's best-friend.

Chapter 6

If It Rains On Vacation, you're Still On Vacation.

"A positive attitude may not solve all your problems, but it will annoy enough people to make it worth the effort."

-Unknown

Vacation: a period of time devoted to travel, recreation, rest and relaxation. Ahh, the word itself can lower the blood pressure of even the most stressed. However, traveling with three kids on family vacations, for me, usually required a recovery period. I did get the travel and recreation part, but not so much the rest and relaxation.

Family vacations, for my own mom and dad, were high on the to-do list of important things. This summer tradition started when I was six and continued though my senior year in high school. I never quite appreciated what my parents did, taking my brother and me on vacation, until I ventured out for the first time as the parent instead of the child.

Jim's brother, Jerry, his wife, Rayanna, and their little girls joined us in Galveston, Texas one August for our first official family vacation.

While we were planning the trip, we never considered the Texas Gulf Coast had just been hit with an offshore oil spill or that 100-degree temperatures and 80 percent humidity with five small children might be as challenging as it was uncomfortable. We were going on vacation!

After our first day at the beach, we stopped at the La Quinta Inn hoping it would fit within our tight travel budget. The guys went inside to check the rates hoping breakfast was included while Rayanna and I stayed in the cars with the sandy-oil-spill-blotched-hot-sweaty-starving kids. I was a nursing mother so I made the necessary adjustments in my wet swimsuit and tee shirt to quiet the hungry baby girl while Travis and Jason used the back seat as a trampoline.

When fifteen minutes or so had passed, Rayanna and I dragged the whole brood into the lobby to find out where our men were and why they left us in the cars to steam like lobsters. Our anger over their thoughtlessness was beginning to brew because we, too, were hungry and sweaty and were dealing with oily sand on us in places where sand shouldn't be. Oh, but we were on vacation!

After a couple of minutes at the counter dealing with a flippant desk clerk, Rayanna looked at me and gasped as if she were taking her last breath. I looked down and instantly prayed that I was having a really bad dream at the same time realizing I was fully awake. I had forgotten I had been nursing the baby and she had fallen asleep. No wonder the clerk wouldn't make eye contact with me! Some of the most wonderful, maybe not fairy-tale wonderful, but memorable things happen on family vacations. It's like being shot out of the classroom straight into the lab of life lessons.

. . . .

Some of the most wonderful, maybe not fairy-tale wonderful, but memorable things happen on family vacations.

. . . .

During one Christmas break, we loaded the three kids in the minivan for the thousand-plus mile road trip to visit my brother and his family in Tampa and take the kids on their first Disney experience. To distract myself from the bickering in the back seat, I thumbed through The Unofficial Guide To Disney World on loan from my friend Kathy. I was discovering all the short cuts to the best rides and where all the bathrooms were located before we even got there. Not considering that the book had sold thousands of copies, I felt like these were secrets no one else had privilege to. When I read the sentence "If you plan to go to the park the week before Easter or the week after Christmas you might as well shoot yourself in the foot," I kept my mouth shut, but mentally started loading the shotgun. Of course we had chosen one of the two busiest times of the year to visit!

As the book so accurately predicted, when we arrived, hoping to meet Mickey and Minnie and their pals, a huge sign was posted: *Sorry, park full to capacity. Come again tomorrow.* You could have scraped the kids up off the asphalt parking lot. Suddenly, in classic Jim Brawner style, he shouted, "That's OK. We're going to Busch Gardens!!" Woo Hoo, we're on vacation!!" Excitement is so contagious that within five minutes Disney World was a foggy memory.

The enormous African animal displays, the rides, shows and food at Busch did not disappoint. Later in the afternoon a typical Florida rain shower caught us off guard two minutes after we had just spent $20.00

on double-dip ice cream cones. "Oh, good grief," I grumbled rolling my eyes while I shook my drenched shirt and wiped ice cream off the seat of my shorts. Seven-year-old Jill quickly reminded me before I could go any further, "It's OK Mom. We're on vacation!"

Of course we were. We had been on many vacations even if there were oil spills and wardrobe malfunctions, even if it was a hundred degrees, even if Disney was maxed out, and even if it rained.

That night, when all five of us were settled in one room, I stared at the ceiling for a long time while everyone else slept. Sure it would have been nice if we had two suites in a five star hotel instead of one room in an economy motel, but who am I to complain. It was vacation! Oh, if only I had that attitude about life as a whole, not just the vacation part. I hate it when I feel guilty like that.

We spend so much time complaining about what we don't have, we forget about what we do have. Being grateful is not a natural phenomenon. It takes awareness and, most of the time, determination. There is just something in all of us that always wants more. And once we get more there is the bigger and better. It's the endless cycle of diminishing returns. The more you get, the more you want because, soon, what you have is just not enough.

• •

We spend so much time complaining about what we don't have, we forget about what we do have.

• •

Romans 12:12 clearly explains how to not get stuck in that cycle and how to take pleasure in the moment. *"Be joyful in hope, patient in affliction and faithful in prayer."* We may not be totally satisfied where we are at this point in time, but we need to enjoy where we are while we are on the way to where we are going.

I have heard young mothers say, "I will be so grateful when she sleeps through the night." "I will be so grateful when she is out of diapers and when she starts school." "I will be so grateful when we are past these preteen years and when she can drive." "I will be so grateful when she is out of school." "I will be grateful when…" Then all of a sudden, the daughter is gone and the young mother is now an older mother who is sad because her daughter is grown. She keeps looking forward to the next stage and, meanwhile, doesn't enjoy the one she's in.

Raising kids is exhausting and sometimes not fun, but we need to learn to dance in the rain while we are waiting for the storm to pass. Maybe that is where the *"patient in affliction"* part of Romans 12:12 comes in. Maybe. Challenging and inconvenient yes, but affliction, I don't know.

One summer we were away from home for four weeks. Not understanding the importance of temperature control, we turned the air conditioner all the way off to save on the electric bill. A friend mowed our lawn and checked on the house once a week. The third week he walked inside the 90-degree house and was literally attacked by sand fleas that had invaded our home. He said the top half of his white socks turned black with fleas. Ugh! To this day, it makes my head itch thinking about it. After several exterminator treatments costing hundreds of dollars, we finally were rid of the fleas. So much for saving money on the electric bill!

Corrie ten Boom in her book The Hiding Place describes the flea infested straw mattresses she and her sister, Betsie, slept on in the Nazi prison camp, Ravensbruck, in 1944. The fleas were so bad the prison guards stayed away from their cell. The blessing of that was they could read their smuggled Bible without being caught and possibly beaten. I think that definitely falls under the *"patient in affliction"* category.

When dogs have fleas they scratch and keep on going. We exterminated our fleas and it was an expensive inconvenience. Corrie and Betsie ten Boom thanked God for their fleas in bona fide affliction! Do you have aggravation fleas, inconvenience fleas or bona fide affliction fleas?

To keep a grateful attitude and avoid the diminishing returns, we need to stay *"joyful in hope."* Things may be rough now, but a mindset of expectant hope will keep you focused. "I know this is not the job I really want, but if I work hard and do the best I can, I know a better one is just around the corner. Meanwhile, I am gong to learn all I can. It's like I am being paid to learn!!" That attitude has a grip on joyful hope and is grateful for the job. Hope is a great expectation of what is to come. Hope will keep you moving forward while enjoying life where you are right now. Hope literally kept Corrie ten Boom alive. Never let hope fade.

. . . .

Things may be rough now, but a mindset of expectant hope will keep you focused.

. . . .

Most importantly we need to stay *"faithful in prayer."* Asking God to keep you mindful of your blessings will help living in the present become a way of life instead of wishing your life away. Thank Him for blessing you. As a parent I know how awesome it was when my kids remembered to thank me for something. Imagine how God feels when we start to develop a grateful heart.

Appreciate everything. We need to get over thinking we always have to be comfortable. When Jason and Travis were little boys, their legs would ache because they were growing so fast. When we aren't being stretched we aren't growing and growth is not usually comfortable. Stay faithful in prayer, thanking the Lord every day for your hundreds of blessings, and watch your attitude start to change.

I think dogs are born grateful creatures. No one trains them to be appreciative. They basically live life as if they have just won an all-expense paid vacation. And their trip never ends. They jump in the car and what's the first thing they do? Stick their heads out the window and feel the breeze and take in all the smells. Let them out in the yard and what do they do? Roll in the grass. Go to the lake? They take off and jump in. And rain doesn't bother them. At all! Why do we scootch along in life just trying to put one foot in front of the other while our dogs are enjoying it to the fullest? That makes me want to stick my head out the window more often.

Where's your focus? If you're obsessing over the door ding, how can you be grateful for your car? Turning sixteen is a huge rite of passage into semi-independence. Several of the new sixteen-year-olds at the high school were showing up in shiny, hip cars while the ink was still wet on their drivers' licenses. After Jason passed his driving test he bought a 1964 Dodge Dart from our family friend, Beverly. It had originally belonged to her gramps and was in mint condition. Grandpa Brown had only driven it 42,000 miles and Jason bought it for $950. Granted driving a Mustang off the show room floor would have been amazing, but Jason was thrilled with the Dart. He was grateful to have a car and content with vintage. And a door ding? Didn't happen. The Dart was built like a tank and was close to invincible. While others were worried about scratches and dirt, Jason was enjoying the ride.

• •

If you are obsessing over the door ding, how can you be grateful for your car?

• •

In the book of Philippians Paul writes, **"...***I have learned to be content whatever the circumstances."* Why is it so hard to be happy with what we have and where we are? We don't always have to have the latest and the newest. Besides, the new wears off pretty fast. I like new things, don't get me wrong, but some things are just better once they are broken in; like shoes and jeans and husbands.

If you have a tough time enjoying what you have or where you are, try making a list of what you are grateful for and appreciate and read it every once in a while. If you honestly can't bring to mind anything you are thankful for, write down things you're glad that you don't have. At least that's a baby step in the right direction. I made a list several years ago and I read it occasionally to jar me back into reality of what's really important. Some of the things on my list are: my family, my health, my friends, a sunset, quiet time in the morning with a cup of hot coffee, the smell of freshly cut grass, God's love, the first day in the fall that you really need a sweater, the first day in the spring that you really don't need a sweater, the smell of a baby's head, a big glass of sweet tea, the voice of one of my kids saying "Hi Mom", puppy breath, the sound of Jim coming in the front door. The older I get, I find I'm grateful I can get up every morning and that wrinkles aren't painful. Sweet, simple things.

It's easier to be grateful when your world is as it should be, but what about when it gets turned upside down. Can you be grateful then? And what is it that throws your life off its axis? Is it just a challenge or truly a huge problem? Most things we face are really just challenges. I'll admit some things are enormous challenges. Can you make the choice to have a challenging day instead of a bad day? Hey, at least you have the day.

• •

It's easier to be grateful when your world is as it should be, but what about when it gets turned upside down.

• •

Not long ago I was in the grocery store checkout line with 20 items or so considering if all the ingredients for dinner were in the cart. As the checker ran the mozzarella cheese across the scanner, I noticed it rang up $1.95 more than the sale sign indicated on the display.

"That cheese is actually on sale for $2.00," I told the twenty-something girl who was ringing up my groceries.

"Oh?" She responded as she pulled out the weekly flyer.

"Well, you are right," she agreed as she motioned to the manager. "Ron, this cheese is on sale and it came up at the regular price."

"I'll be right back," he said heading toward the far corner of the store to the dairy case.

Feeling inconsiderate for slowing down the late afternoon flow of the checkout line, I turned to the woman behind me and apologized for the computer error. She smiled politely probably wondering how she always ends up behind someone who wants a price check or debates with the clerk over coupons. Ron returned explaining I had picked up the 16-ounce package, not the 12-ounce package that was on sale. As he handed me the cheese, I turned to the woman behind me again. This time I was not expecting to receive such a pleasant smile since it was my human error instead of the computer.

"I am so sorry," I said to her, embarrassed. "I know how irritating it is to be in line behind shoppers like me."

Since frustration with other people's mistakes is not easily hidden at five o'clock in the afternoon, her response surprised me.

She grinned and said, "I refuse to let four ounces of cheese ruin my otherwise wonderful day."

That should be inscribed in stone somewhere! Because I had picked up the wrong package of cheese was, for her, a simple mistake, not something to spin her world out of control.

Have you ever watched a three-year-old throw a fit over circumstances? Usually you have to let him wear himself down to the point of exhaustion. Then, and only then, can you reason with him. I think that's exactly what God does with us. He let's us wear ourselves out with our fit throwing until we are so tired we will finally listen to Him. If we were gut-level honest about it, perceiving we constantly have problems and always complaining might just might be a sign of immaturity. I'll have to admit on some days it's easy to be mature and on other days I'm not so grown up. We really need to stop murmuring and complaining.

Besides what does that fix and who wants to listen to it? Lets face it: every one of us is in the midst of trials. Really we are either about to enter a trial, are in the middle of one, or are coming out on the other side of one. Essentially, trails are inevitable; hissy fits are optional.

Rin Tin Tin and Lassie were remarkable TV hero dogs. Even awkward, clumsy Scooby Doo managed to, in spite of himself, save the day. God gave us this life to enjoy and live to the fullest. Are you the victim or the hero of your life story? Victims murmur, heroes don't. Victims complain, heroes say thank you. Victims say "if only" heroes look at the possibilities and say "what if." Victims whine about the rain, heroes splash in the puddles. The Lord sets our path but we choose how to walk it. Once we make the shift away from murmuring and complaining, moving toward gratefulness will be like going from black and white to color. So, if it rains on your vacation, remember it's still vacation. Besides, there's always the possibility of a rainbow.

Chapter 7

Leave The Drama To Hollywood

"Poise is the knack of raising your eyebrows instead of the roof."

-Unknown

I worked in several different areas of the entertainment industry for ten years. The glamorous facade of Hollywood began to fade about three months after I started.

My agent called. "Jill, I booked a job for you on a skit with Jon Stewart for the Emmys. Filming starts tomorrow at 6am. Go to the Entertainment Tonight studio. Here's the address. Don't be a minute late!" she instructed.

Excited, I hung up the phone and called everyone I knew to announce I was going to be on the Emmy Awards show with Jon Stewart. So jazzed up, I only slept two hours that night. I arrived at the studio an hour early just to make sure I wasn't a minute late.

When I entered the lobby of the tall, slick New York City building a security guard greeted me at the front desk. I guess he recognized me from a picture because without introductions he said, "Miss Brawner, are you ready for me to escort you to the studio?"

Trying to act as if I had done this dozens of times, I said, "Yes, we can go up now." When I got up stairs, even though I was early, a production assistant hurried me along saying, "Jill, they are ready for you in make-up".

I assumed the room with bright lights was the make up room so I went on in. Jon Stewart in the make-up chair. "You must be Jill," he smiled.

"You must be Jon," I said grinning.

"Well, sit down and we will run over the script while we get our make up done," he said.

As we went over the lines, he put me at ease with his causal approach. We ran the scene for the cameras at least thirty times. It must have been good because we made the director laugh. When we finished, I said goodbye and shook hands with Jon like I was a veteran. I said, "It was nice working with you today, Jon." Thanks, Jill. You too. Great job! You kicked butt!"

I left the studio on a cloud. That was awesome!

The Emmy Awards were the next week so I flew home to be with family and friends to watch my big two-minute television debut. I was thrilled. We all gathered at a friend's house for dinner and to watch the show. Jon Stewart was host that year and the pre-taped skits with him were used as fillers and introductions throughout the evening. Everyone was anxiously waiting for the big moment.

About half–way through the show the skit finally started. Jon was in the middle of his monologue and everyone knew my big entrance was coming. My arm came onto the scene and…. CUT! They had edited my big debut! Everyone screamed, "AHH!"

I had just learned my first lesson about the industry; nothing is for sure until you see it. Edits and cuts are sometimes even made during a show. I discovered it was best to let others tell me they had seen me instead of announcing that I was going to be seen. Even what seemed to be the best dramatic scene could be trimmed and or even totally eliminated.

• •

I had just learned my first lesson about the industry; nothing is for sure until you see it.

• •

Working in such a strange field, over the years I have learned so much, especially about human nature. People in the industry are fascinating, but really have nothing over the general public. The only difference is the tabloids and the paparazzi. We are all so different which makes for a real life blockbuster. There is a little bit of drama in all of us.

• •

There is a little bit of drama in all of us.

• •

I was in the Dallas/Fort Worth airport on my way home after an event. Springtime in Texas is famous for thunderstorms, so I just mentally pre-plan for at least a 2 hour delay if I'm flying through there that time of year. All the business people were ready to hop on a plane and make the next deal. This particular Monday seemed to be extra busy and, as I expected, a lot of the flights were delayed due to rough weather.

The terminal was crawling with suits on their phones franticly trying to reschedule meetings. One man in particular was becoming irate

73

walking back and forth in the gate area. His voice grew louder as his frustration level crept upward with each call he made. For some strange reason, he chose me to dump all his problems on.

He ranted and raved about how ridiculous American Airlines was. They were always overly cautious. All the other airlines were flying right now in the thunderstorms. Why weren't we? He explained to me that he had a big meeting that would take his company to the next level if he were able to close the deal. He had one shot to pitch his proposal and this was it. It had taken a full 18 months just to get the meeting. I simply nodded my head with a conjured up look of concern on my face. Acting classes do come in handy.

He continued pacing back and forth between the seat next to me and the gate agent as if doing that would make the weather move out faster. I'm sure the gate agent was as anxious as he was for the plane to take off. He asked repeatedly about the new estimated departure time. She assured him each time as soon as the captain thought it was clear and safe we would take off. With every passing minute he became more and more agitated. I was beginning to believe he might become a candidate for a visit from security or from the paramedics with treatment for a heart attack.

Finally, after another 30 minutes passed, the agent announced, "We have good news. We are able to proceed with boarding but we are going to have to change gates. Please make sure you have all of your belongings and proceed to gate B-12"

At this point my irritated traveling buddy had worked himself up into such a tizzy he was at the point of causing a huge scene. He threw his hands in the air and said, "This is total persecution!"

Now, this is the point on a movie set the director yells, "Cut!" because the actor has gotten a little too dramatic. Unfortunately this scene was in real life and not on a stage.

Total persecution? Come on! I had had enough. He was driving everyone crazy! He's was a least thirty years my senior, but I began to think this is what it must feel like to travel with an obnoxious younger sibling. Since I was on a first name basis with the guy, I felt I had earned the right to act as the real life director and in some way let him know he was over-acting in this scene.

"Sam, my friend Ruth survived the holocaust in Germany during the war," I started. "She could possibly tell you what persecution looks like. A delayed flight and a potently missed business deal isn't persecution! It just is what it is. We are all sorry for you and as unfortunate as your situation is, it doesn't fall anywhere near the definition of persecution," I said with the conviction of a politician.

As fellow passengers were agreeing with head nods and mouthing "thank you", Sam surprised us all by saying, "I'm sorry." He finally calmed down and shut up.

I wish I could say that my behavior has always been above reproach and that I've never reacted like Sam, but that's not true. If each one of us took an assessment of how we have treated others and the scenes we have created, an award-winning movie could be produced.

• •

If each one of us took an assessment of how we have treated others and the scenes we have created, an award-winning movie could be produced.

• •

75

Being the typical baby of the family and the only girl, I was the obvious target for mischief that Jason and Travis dreamed up. And, oh were they creative knowing exactly how to push my buttons. When I would end up in a total nuclear melt down over no telling what, they would bring out the video camera.

Jason would pose as the director and Travis the cameraman. They would chase me all over the house as I screamed and cried and occasionally fell to the floor for special effects. Jason would say, "Ok, that's good. Now more drama... Good!"

Then Travis would ask for more emotion, "Could you cry a little more for the camera? Oh, let's move to the other room because the lighting is just not right in here."

It didn't take long until the act was over. I didn't want to give them the satisfaction of the response they were looking for and I realized how ridiculous I looked. To add insult to injury they would play it back on TV as if it was a world premiere. They would hold their sides laughing. And I would too. It always ended up being fun for all three of us and I would forget why I was so distressed to begin with. My brothers knew the drama was in me.

Children are literally trained by responses to their fits. My brothers saw my behavior as absolutely unacceptable. They didn't ignore me, but their technique to stop my meltdowns worked. I wonder if Sam from the airport had always had those around him tripping over themselves to appease him when he got wound up. Just like a kid, reinforced behaviors in adults will more than likely be repeated. Dramatic scene-causing adults are really big kids who haven't emotionally grown up.

• •

Dramatic scene-causing adults are really big kids who haven't emotionally grown up.

• •

Maybe some of us never really leave Jr. High, emotionally anyway. Drama is selfish, self centered and self-serving. It's all-about-me behavior yearning to draw attention. It's as if a flashing neon arrow needs to follow these people. Some play the damsel in distress in the story of their own life. It's cute for Rapunzel, but it looks ridiculous in reality. Are you guilty of writing in unnecessary drama in your life story?

We all know those who are continually in the middle of turmoil. If their life hits a smooth spot it's almost uncomfortable and they are capable of stirring up chaos to get back their unsettled normal. The challenge is to stay out of their soap opera. Don't get drawn in as a character. What happens when you're in the company of these people is you tend to mirror their behavior even though your feelings aren't necessarily on that track. It's so emotionally conflicting. If you have to jump on the Ferris wheel, circle only once and hop off as soon as you can.

According to 2 Timothy 1:7 God gave us a spirit of love, discipline and a sound mind. Are you using the mind God gave you or are you just blending into the white noise of the background and being sucked into surrounding chaos?

My first day of acting class at a New York conservatory, the teacher explained it was going to be three really intense hours each time we met. She went on to say we needed to come to class with a clear mind

77

and we must be able to give ourselves some recovery time after class. All the work would be highly emotional.

Wow, I had no idea what I had signed up for. I wouldn't be able to sleep after her class because my emotions would be rung dry. Even though I was exhausted, my eyes wouldn't close. My brain just wouldn't shut off. If my body responded to pretend drama in that way, just think what the real thing can do. No wonder we are so worn out after a real life drama.

• •

If my body responded to pretend drama in that way, just think what the real thing can do. No wonder we are so worn out after a real life drama.

• •

There is a time and place for drama. It's fun to watch it, but hard on us to live it. It can wreak havoc in our lives and the lives of those around us. According to the American Heart Association over 72 million people in the United States age 20 and older have high blood pressure. Granted, eating and exercise habits and genetics have a tremendous role in that statistic, but I wonder how much out of control emotions or drama adds to it. An out of balance perception of our circumstances can slowly be killing us. Stress can compromise our ability to fight off disease and infection, throw our digestive system off balance, make it difficult to conceive a baby, and can even stunt growth in children. It is so powerful.

Just think how much money could be saved every year on blood pressure medication alone if we left the drama to the professionals. Proverbs 14:30 confirms it. "A heart at peace gives life to the body…"

One minor shift in the way we react to circumstances is good for our health.

One morning my dog Bro and I were on a walk through Beverly Hills. Dogs are pretty funny in Beverly Hills. Most of them are groomed weekly and have outfits that cost more than a round trip ticket to Hawaii. It's quite a scene. Some of the girl dogs look like they should be wearing high heels and carrying a small purse.

All I wanted was a nice cup of coffee and a quite place to sit and read with the un-groomed Bro at my side. It's amazing how a dog can keep you company. He was very social and loved to go out with me every chance he gets. Bro was a white Labrador retriever and would have probably rather be sniffing around in the woods but he seemed to enjoy the sidewalk smells and the leftover crumbs outside the little cafes.

As we approached one of my favorite outdoor coffee and muffin cafes, I spotted the perfect table. It was a beautiful day and my plan to sip on a latte and read my novel was coming together perfectly. As Bro and I crossed the street, I notice a beautiful Lassie-looking dog sitting perfectly behaved right at her owner's side. She was so lady-like and seemed to be enjoying the weather and company of the rest of the patrons. Her leash was tied in a perfect bow right around the base of the small bistro table where her owner was reading the Los Angeles Times and sipping his foamy cappuccino.

Just as we walked up to be seated, Bro must have caught Lady Lassie's eye and you would have thought a teenage girl had just seen the lead singer of her favorite rock band. She went ballistic barking in a weird high-pitched whine! I guess it was some sort of seductive dog flirting voice. Most dogs in that neighborhood are fixed to help keep some peace and social order so this behavior was really strange.

The owner tried to calm her down without much success. Fixed or not this girl was hot after Bro. In one giant leap she flipped over the bistro table she was perfectly tied to and silverware, food, glasses and cappuccino went flying everywhere. A nicely dressed women sitting at the next table was now covered in foam and black coffee.

"Sidney!" her owner yelled as she bolted toward Bro with the table still tied to her. I realized we needed to exit quickly to avoid further destruction. My plan didn't work. I hurried Bro, but Sydney turned and was trailing us with the bistro table hanging on for dear life behind her. I think Bro was a little freaked out by her at this point because he sped up to a slow jog and tucked his tail between his legs. I looked back and to my shock she was gaining on us, bistro table and all. Bro looked at me as if to say, "Get me out of here. This broad is nuts!"

The distressed owner yelled, "Sidney, stop! Sydney stop!" Finally the crazed dog came to her senses and sat down as the table swung around and almost knocked someone over. We kept on moving. I waved at the guy in a shrugging manner. What could I have said: "I'm sorry my dog is so good looking that he caused a scene?" Sometimes it's best to just say nothing!

Sydney might have benefited from high blood pressure meds. I was really proud of Bro for keeping his cool. I learned a lot from him that morning. When we ignore irrational behavior and remove ourselves from a tense situation, things usually will calm down. If we want things around us to be in control, we have to stay in control. Counting to ten helps. Sometimes counting to 100 is even better.

• •

If we want things around us to be in control, we have to stay in control.

• •

There are a lot of talented dogs in movies, on TV and in commercials. The "Yo Quiero Taco Bell" dog was one of my all time favorites. He looked so serious about Mexican fast food. It's amazing to me how they can be trained to act. Jason even taught his 150-pound English mastiff to get down on his belly and Rambo along the floor like he was dodging bullets in some covert operation. He didn't even live in Hollywood!

The word peace is used countless times in Scripture. Peace is not the absence of chaos, but it's having the ability to remain calm in the midst of the chaos. Our world is chaotic, that's a given. Drama surrounds us. It's almost impossible to escape it. It's powerful to understand we have a choice to audition for a dramatic role or leave the drama to Hollywood.

Chapter 8

My Reality And Your Reality Aren't The Same

"When the game is over, the king and pawn go back in the same box."

-Unknown

I was the speaker for a destination weekend church retreat. A four-star hotel was a three-day escape for 75 or so women. Besides the speaker sessions and roundtable discussions, spa pampering, Food Channel worthy meals, and catching up with friends were all on the agenda. The weekend also included free time to shop or simply to catch up on some much needed sleep. Many of these women rarely had the chance to visit except over bleachers at ball games or in parking lots while collecting kids from activities. Needless to say, it was going to be one big girlfriend sleepover.

After I reviewed the schedule for the weekend, doubt and fear began to creep in like cockroaches as I wondered how I was going to be as exciting and inspiring as pedicures and chocolate. "No one cares who the speaker is and what she has to say," I murmured to myself. "Clearly these women are just glad to be away."

This event had become an annual affair held the same weekend for the last 10 years. Many of those attending had known each other since grade school. This particular year, though, the leadership had decided to invite another church to join them, so several potential new friends were in the mix.

An elegant four-course dinner on china and white linens was first on the program Friday evening. The finishing touch for each woman was a butter cream frosted individual cake topped with a fresh white lily. It was served with specialty coffees in little flowered cups and saucers. The women's ministry director explained the options for the evening while forks quietly clicked on the dessert plates. Giggles and light conversation left no doubt this was a girls-only weekend. I smiled knowing this was, most likely, the first uninterrupted meal many had experienced, maybe, since last year's retreat.

After dinner the neck and shoulder massage and a hot bath at the spa were as good as *Raid!* chasing out the uncertainty of my competence as the speaker. After all, I was invited, I remembered as I headed for the white down comforter already turned back in my room. There was one thing I absolutely had no doubt about; these women understood the full meaning of retreat.

• •

There was one thing I absolutely had no doubt about; these women understood the full meaning of retreat.

• •

Saturday morning after a breakfast of Eggs Benedict and fresh fruit we went to roundtable discussions. Since there were several first-timers and women from the other church, the leadership had planned get to know you mixers. Building community was one of their goals for the retreat. I was assigned to a table with four girls who had been to the weekend most of the last 10 years and Lisa, who was there for the very first time. Everyone, including Lisa, knew each other. While I was just trying to remember names, they were catching up on important things like who had signed up to teach vacation Bible school and their friend Michelle's pending divorce.

After instructions, questions were passed to the tables for discussion. Our first question was, "Where is the most interesting place you have ever lived?" It was fascinating to hear where these women had been. One woman's parents were missionaries, so she had spent her childhood in Africa. Because her father was in the military, another had lived in four different countries while she was growing up. As my turn was nearing, I still didn't know how I to answer. I had always lived in Arkansas or Missouri. Beautiful, safe, routine, but interesting, I'm not so sure. Then I suddenly remembered a very interesting place I had lived: a fifth wheel camper trailer. That should count!

I began by explaining when we moved to Branson years ago, the boom hadn't hit yet so available housing was not as it is now. We were in the process of building a house and needed a place to rent for only six months. Most of the landlords didn't want to rent to people with children or pets. Since we had three kids and a big dog, we were turned down again and again.

Finally, a friend offered his camper trailer that hooked into the bed of a truck for towing. It was too small to sleep all five of us so we pulled up and parked it next to a cabin that wasn't winterized. Jim wired up an intercom between the cabin and the trailer so we could at least hear what was going on with the kids. The trailer had a kitchen, a sleeping loft and a primitive bathroom of sorts. The cabin had a bunk bed with a trundle and another bathroom of sorts. I was mortified that I had my three kids living like this. They, however, thought it was an adventure and Jim finally had his opportunity to be a real mountain man. None of this seemed to faze Josie, our dog. Her only concern was that she was with us.

If the bathroom was occupied, it was not a problem for the boys. We lived in the woods! The shower was so small it even hit ten-year-old Jason in the chest. Because the temperatures had dipped into the twenties, when I went to the cabin one morning to wake the kids for school, I found them asleep in their snowsuits! I was certain if anyone found this out, the authorities would be called. I could barely raise half-hearted sympathy as the women laughed at my story knowing my situation was only temporary. Everyone did agree, though, I truly had lived in an interesting place!

. . . .

I could barely raise half-hearted sympathy as the women laughed at my story knowing my situation was only temporary.

. . . .

Sitting next to me, Lisa was the last to answer. She attended the invited church, but knew everyone at the table and had since she, her husband and two boys had moved from another part of the state ten years earlier. She taught second grade and her husband was a nurse at the local hospital. They were a well-known and respected family in the community.

She took a deep breath before she answered the question. "I am so grateful you invited the women from our church to join you this year," she began looking around the table. "I really needed a break and this is way beyond my expectations. The food, the wonderful spa and the heavenly beds are something at one point in my life I only could read and dream about. You see the most interesting place I have ever lived was in a car with my mother. For two years, when I was in high school, we were homeless. When Dad died Mom and I ended up losing everything, " she said. "I guess a car counts as unusual as well as interesting."

"Oh, good grief, Lisa," one girl blurted out. I consider us to be good friends and I didn't know that. How on earth did you make it?"

"We took showers in roadside parks and campgrounds and took care of ourselves the best way we could," she smiled. "Mom insisted I stay in school, so I never missed a day while she took on all the work she could. It was very hard to say the least. I clung to the scripture in first Peter that says "Humble yourselves, therefore, under God's mighty hand, that He may lift you up in due time. Cast you anxiety on Him because He cares for you."

"Some days it was really difficult to believe He really cared for me, or even think He knew I existed, but guess what, in due time He lifted me up. And I have been blessed more than I could have ever imagined. It's been fifteen years now, but I am still amazed when I have the opportunity to come to events like this. I'll never take anything for granted, that's for sure."

I literally felt as if God had just whispered in my ear like a parent quietly trying to get a kid's attention.

• •

I literally felt as if God had just whispered in my ear like a parent quietly trying to get a kid's attention.

• •

Lisa's reality and my reality were worlds apart. I chose to live in a camper trailer. Lisa didn't choose to live in a car. As frustrating and inconvenient as it was, I knew I would be moving into a beautiful new home at the end of six months. Lisa barely clung to a thread of hope that she would some day move out of the back seat of a car. How could I become so near sighted that I don't look past my circumstances to try to understand others? Was I that selfish? That was tough to chew on and really hard to swallow! I felt like I left that weekend having learned so much more than I had taught.

We get so busy wrapped up in our own little worlds we think everyone should experience life as we do. Even though we live on the same earth, we see the horizon differently. What does it mean to have a tough day? Having a flat tire on the car with a broken air conditioner while driving from her day job to her night job constitutes a hard day for one person. Smudging a fresh manicure while struggling to load packages from Neiman Marcus into the SUV is a rough day for someone else. Even though they might only live a few miles apart, the world looks totally different to these two women. It would be hard for each of them to understand what life is like for the other.

• •

Even though we live on the same earth, we see the horizon differently.

• •

I'm amazed at how Amy handles six kids. Raising three pushed my limits. I can't imagine taking care of an adult child who was born with extreme handicaps. Pam handled it with grace. The thought of being diagnosed with Leukemia is mind-boggling to me. Roxanne battles it with a beautiful smile. Janelle's husband Gregg's passion is to fly airplanes, ride motorcycles, bike across country and travel all over the world. Life with him must be like living in a Mountain Dew commercial. I get tired just thinking about it. I can't imagine myself living in any of my friends' shoes.

Looking up out of our own circumstances helps us develop a sense of empathy. Sympathy is just expressing sorrow for the pain or distress for someone else. Empathy is a transfer of your own feelings or emotions to someone else. It's like mentally putting on their shoes for a while... even if it's taking off your flip-flops and putting on some Jimmy Choos.

• •

Looking up out of our own circumstances helps us develop a sense of empathy.

• •

We are all so different and that makes life challenging. But the fact we are different is also what brings balance. If we were all the same the earth would become lopsided like an overloaded washing machine. God had a purpose in that plan I am quite certain. It would be so boring otherwise. We aren't supposed to figure it out; we're just supposed to love and encourage one another.

The problem comes when we start to compare ourselves with everyone else. When we do, jealousy, fear and envy begin to sneak in. In 1

Corinthians 13, the love chapter, it very clearly says, "love does not envy."

I saw a TV interview with Marlo Thomas several years ago. The host asked Marlo, "What is one of the most important things you have ever been told?"

She answered with a story of the first acting job she had in a summer playhouse years ago.

"At seventeen I was thrilled to get the part. The morning after opening night I was excited to read the reviews. The critics were so kind and the reviews were stellar. However, the one thing that ran through every article was the comparison of me to my Dad. Would I be as good as my dad, would I last as long as my dad, would I be as funny as my dad... I read it over and over. Yikes, how could anyone compare to Danny Thomas even if I was his daughter! I called my dad and explained my frustration. I even threatened to change my last name because I could never live up to it."

My dad laughed and said, "Marlo, listen to me. I raised a thoroughbred. Do you know what thoroughbreds do? They get in the racing stall with their blinders on and run their race as hard as they can. They are not concerned about all the other horses and what they are doing. They are focused on the track ahead of them."

That had a huge impact on me. The next day when I was in my dressing room getting ready for the show, a stagehand knocked on the door and handed me a big box with a bow on it. I opened it and inside was a pair of old horse binders and a note from my dad that said, "Run your own race, baby."

I think that's what all of us need to do. Stop comparing ourselves to everyone else and focus on our own race. That would hold off envy and jealousy for sure.

It's so easy to be critical and judgmental. Everyone has an opinion. When you begin to establish ideas or opinions consider what you are building them on. If you think about it, judgment is based solely on our own standards, our own reality - whatever that might be. Forming an opinion about something we have no experience with is not fair. We are quick to judge, but how quick are we to love? We are quick to position ourselves higher than others, but how quick are we to put their shoes on and walk in empathy.

• •

If you think about it, judgment is based solely on our own standards, our own reality - whatever that might be.

• •

One of the most powerful things I have ever realized is the foot of The Cross is level ground. Our roads to get there may really look quite different, but once we arrive, it doesn't matter. We are each uniquely special and important to God. Acts 10:34 says, *"I now realize how true it is that God does not show favoritism, but accepts men from every nation who fear Him and do what is right."* We need to be careful to never get to the point where we think we understand everything and know it all. That is like riding a skateboard down hill heading right toward gravel.

Proverbs 16:18 clearly explains, *"Pride goes before destruction, a haughty spirit before a fall"*. At the center of grace and humility is where we need to sit. Why do we focus on all of the external trapping of our faith and live with a punch list of things we think we must do while forgetting what's really important? *"Love the Lord your God with all your heart and with all your soul and with all your mind. This is the first and greatest commandment. And the second is like it: love your neighbor as yourself."* Matthew 22:37-39. It doesn't' matter what our individual worlds look like, we are called to honor, respect and love each other even though your reality and my reality aren't the same. My responsibility is to run the race set before me and love my neighbor while I'm circling the track.

Not too long ago I sat and watched the dog of a homeless man who lived on the beach in southern California. She had a red bandana around her neck. A nicely dress woman and her fussy little dog with a fancy collar and leash and designer doggy sweater prissed by. I'm quite certain the homeless dog wasn't thinking, "Shoot, I wish I had a collar like that. Oh, that sweater is to die for." Truly she wasn't concerned that she didn't live in a five-bedroom, four-bath home in the right neighborhood. It didn't look like it really bothered her that she was having someone's leftover hamburger instead of prime cut Alpo for dinner. Her focus seemed to be on loving her master. It's as if, in some strange, way she understood Micah 6:8 - *"And what does the Lord require of you? Act justly, love mercy, and walk humble wit your God."* ...Be nice, extend plenty of grace, and hang out with God, regardless of the circumstances.

Chapter 9

What's Hiding In Your Purse?

"Life is an adventure in forgiveness."

-Norman Cousins

Juggling life raising three kids, I always tried to figure out how to do things as efficiently as possible. Consequently, for years my purse was more functional than stylish. I always needed one of everything, so the more stuff it held the better it was. It not only carried my things, but whatever anyone in my family handed me landed in my purse, too. I ended up in the doctor's office once with chronic neck and shoulder pain. The diagnosis? Stop lugging around ten pounds of junk over your shoulder and the pain should stop. I spent $75 and two hours to be told I needed to carry a smaller, ladylike purse.

On one occasion, while rummaging for a pen, I found a half eaten Happy Meal hamburger wrapped in a napkin at the bottom of my purse. I was relieved when I realized the almost petrified snack couldn't have been in there more than seven days because I had just bought the purse the week before. That might be giving myself too much credit, though, as it could have been transferred with all the other junk from the old purse. I choose to believe the seven-day theory.

For years my friend, Mary, has carried one of those tiny eight- inch by six-inch organizer purses with a skinny little strap that has a slot and zippered pouch for everything you really need. It's one of those doctor-recommended ladylike purses. Last Christmas, her adult children gave her a beautiful, soft leather, expensive purse. It's almost the size of an airline-approved carry on bag. They felt she needed to make a change in her purse carrying style. She loves her ladylike purse, but she didn't want to offend her children so she carries the new purse with her little purse in it. There's nothing else in there, just her little purse.

Once, at a weekend retreat, I learned a lot about what women haul around. One of the icebreakers the first night was a game using only purses to find a list of items. Teams consisted of 10 women. I don't remember junior high youth group scavenger hunts being this competitive. Jumping, shouting women were throwing things from all angles. It was great fun and honestly quite stress relieving. Our team laughed so hard half of us had to head to the ladies room.

. . . .

We hang on to hurt feelings, anger, bitterness,
and unforgiveness, hiding them in the little
zippered compartments of our ladylike purses
or dragging them around in oversized bags that
send us to the doctor with shoulder and neck pain.

. . . .

The next morning we were in discussion groups mulling over thought-provoking questions. The mood was much more serious than the night before as each woman shared hidden little corners of her soul. As we took turns around the table the, discussion seemed to go deeper and deeper.

The last to share in our small group was a vibrant, beautiful woman who reminded me of one of those popular girls in high school you were secretly jealous of because she always wore the right thing and always said the right thing. Elaine definitely had it together. As she spoke, no one moved a muscle.

"There's a big age gap between my older siblings and me. I like to think of myself as a pleasant surprise," she started with a slight grin. "One Christmas, being the precious little one, I was showered with gifts from my parents. My teen-aged siblings, on the other hand, each received only one gift beautifully wrapped with a big bow on top. Inside each box was a letter from our mother. It read: This Christmas you aren't receiving any gifts. Instead you are getting this letter. It's in exchange for every time you disobeyed me, every time you didn't finish what you started and every time you disappointed me.

There was an uncomfortable silence around the table. I suddenly realized why there was severe pain in my chest. I wasn't breathing. I finally blinked and took a breath as I felt like this beautiful had-it-all-together woman was acting out a script from a B grade horror movie. Amazingly she continued on, "You know what the saddest part of it all is?"

There's more and it gets sadder? Impossible!!

"My sister has carried that letter around in her purse all these years," she finished as big tears leaked down her cheeks.

Unbelievable! That was too much hurt for me to process. This sweet woman was hurting for her sister, her siblings, her mother and for herself.

I thought about Elaine's story for several days finally realizing that we all carry things around with us. We hang on to hurt feelings, anger, bitterness, and unforgiveness, hiding them in the little zippered compartments of our ladylike purses or dragging them around in oversized bags that send us to the doctor with shoulder and neck pain. Why do we clutch on so tightly? Maybe we feel like we are holding something over our offenders. In reality we are the ones who are suffering under the load. It's as if the offense will be lessened if we forgive and go on, so, by golly, we are going to stay angry and stew in it. Colossians 3:13 encourages us to *"Bear with each other and forgive whatever grievances you may have against one another. Forgive as the Lord forgave you."*

I read once that clinging to anger and unforgiveness is like putting acid in a can for use at a later time. Meanwhile the acid is eating away at the vessel it's stored in. If you are hiding away anger you might as well paint a skull-and-crossbones on your forehead. Poison inside! It eats away at us mentally, emotionally, spiritually, and physically. Do we stockpile all the anger and rage to have just in case the opportunity comes up to unload a surprise attack on our offender? What good does that do? What's really interesting is we don't stop to consider the one who has hurt us is many times oblivious to the fact that he or she has stomped on our hearts.

That very thing happened to me years ago when a friend offended me terribly. I spent two years with a knot as tight as wet rope in the pit of my stomach every time I was around this thoughtless person. Finally

I realized it was my choice to do something about the situation. He certainly wasn't going to. Over coffee I explained the reason for the meeting and I asked for forgiveness for harboring horrible feelings toward him. He sat with his mouth gaping like the Disney hound dog character, Goofy, as I recounted the offense from two years earlier.

"I had no idea you were hurt! Can you forgive me for being so thoughtless," he asked. "I guess I'm just bumbling along in life trying to do the best I can."

"Sure I can forgive you," I said, as it occurred to me that I'm also just bumbling along and hoped I, too, hadn't deeply hurt someone unknowingly.

The saddest part was I had wasted two years of energy on a misunderstanding.

My shoulder instantly felt relief as I took that load out of my purse.

What really hit me in the head that day was everyone who offends me is not a nasty, evil person whose mission is to make my life miserable. People are human and are going to offend, most of the time, unaware. True, there are the inherently mean who do the best they can to purposefully hurt. They are like the scorpion I came across that was swinging it's pinchers back and forth as it traveled along the ground hitting whatever got in it's way. I watched in amazement wondering why it was so agitated. Over time I have learned to feel nothing but sadness for the perpetually angry. Their exhausting load has to be painful cargo.

• •

People are human and are going to offend, most of the time,
unaware.

• •

Not only does anger harden your looks and cause health issues, it can totally destroy relationships. So many times those around you who have nothing to do with your emotional eruptions are the ones who frequently suffer. Someone who may innocently step on your last nerve - kicking up simmering to boiling-over - will bear the consequences of your anger even when he or she isn't the real cause. Blindsiding like that can eat away at the foundation of a relationship like a charging herd of termites!

Taking a closer look, I began to realize I should also consider why I get offended. Do I need to extend some much-needed grace to bulldozer people who run over my feelings? Is my vision so narrow all I can see is myself and how I feel? Poor little me! I am so hurt! Jill said to me once when I was whining about my hurt feelings, "Mom, you have a choice. You can pout or you can go to Lowe's, buy some lumber, build a bridge, and get on over it!!"

That stung a little, but she was right. I do have a choice and it's up to me when construction begins. Sometimes I have to rework the bridge blueprints if I choose to hang on to hurt, but eventually I walk on over the bridge. It's so much easier to live on the other side of anger.

Because of the damage that's been done, sometimes it may take years of working through the hurt and healing the wounds before forgiveness can happen. Ephesians 4:31 says, *"Get rid of all bitterness, rage, and anger, brawling and slander, along with every form of malice".* In other words, lighten your load. Until we do, we are like the scorpion swinging our pinchers lashing out hitting whatever gets in our way.

• •

Because of the damage that's been done, sometimes it may take years of working through the hurt and healing the wounds before forgiveness can happen..

• •

I am sure there are countless ways to work through hurt and anger and start the forgiveness process but these few things seem to work and make the most sense for me. First, consider the source of your anger or hurt. Awareness is key. If it is something you have power to change, go to work on it. If it is something you can't change, start bridge construction as soon as possible. The bridge may be as simple as putting large rocks in a creek to tiptoe across, keeping you out of the mud; or it might be as complicated as constructing the Brooklyn Bridge made of concrete and steel taking you across a river with life-threatening currents. As you start, pray for the courage and strength to begin the journey, then ask for wisdom to draw up your mental blueprints. Being the borderline control fanatic that I am, once I realized that I was actually giving up command of my emotions to someone else when I stayed angry, I couldn't get over the bridge fast enough. Don't let someone else hold you captive when freedom is only a decision away.

Second: Do you keep a running ledger of offenses people commit? If so, stop it now! It uses up way too much valuable brain space in the memory bank and each time a person doesn't measure up to your expectations, anger builds. Once, when asked about an offense committed against her, Mother Teresa responded, "Oh, yes, I specifically remember forgetting that." Oh, to be so gracious!

Hebrews 12:15 says to *"Watch out that no poisonous root of bitterness grows up to trouble you, corrupting many."* Starting a ledger plants the seed and each entry adds fertilizer to the root. Roots can grow deep and are hard to get rid of. I was pulling some weeds in Kari and Travis' flowerbed in Oklahoma one summer and came across a mushroom like plant. When I tried to pull it out it wouldn't budge. I turned up one corner and there were probably seventy-five roots growing down from the underside of the plant choking out everything beneath it. It was disgusting!! I realized two things: strange stuff grows in the Oklahoma red dirt and that is probably what the root of bitterness looks like. Throw out your ledger if you keep one. It's nothing but bitterness root fertilizer.

First Corinthians thirteen, the love chapter, is read at countless weddings. The second part of verse five says, referring to love…*"it is not easily angered, it keeps no record of wrongs."* In the midst of all the white fluff and flowers, do we really listen to those words and think about what they really mean. I'm fully convinced the reason over half of marriages in the US today unravel is because we keep ledgers. Long, detailed ledgers.

• •

I'm fully convinced the reason over half of marriages in the US today unravel is because we keep ledgers. Long, detailed ledgers.

• •

Years ago, early in our marriage, Jim did something that made me so mad I couldn't see straight. Right before dinner that night when I was in the kitchen, he said, "Suz, I know I am a dummy. I am so sorry for what I said this morning. The problem is I will probably continue to make thoughtless mistakes throughout our marriage. Can you forgive me?"

How do you say no to that? "Of course I can and l will."

He continued, "I brought you something to remind you that you forgave me once and I'll need a lot more grace and forgiveness over the years." He handed me a small block of wood with 70 x 7 printed on it. That, of course, is the answer Jesus gave when asked how many times we are to forgive. It still sits by my kitchen sink today. It's a reminder for me that forgiveness is continual and ledger keeping prevents forgiveness.

The third way to walk toward forgiveness is to stop rehashing. By that I mean stop going over and over and over the offense in your mind or by retelling your story. Each time it's told, the details only grow uglier. I heard a pastor once liken rehashing to replaying a DVD again and again. We continue to hit replay when what we really need to do is hit eject. There is no way to edit yesterday so we might as well give up the hope that there is any way it could be different. Learn from it, eject and move on.

So, here's a starting point. Build a bridge and walk over it, throw out the ledger and eject the DVD. You'll feel so much better! These are three approaches to the journey out of anger and unforgiveness. However, the best possible thing to do is to just avoid the boggy mess that sucks your energy dry and pulls you down.

Romans 12:8 says, *"As far as it depends on you, live at peace with everyone."* The key words are "as it depends on you." Remember, you have absolutely no control over anyone but yourself. You will be waiting one long time if you're depending on the people around you to bring peace into your life.

Again, the choice is yours. Once I realized anger prevention was up to me, this simple idea changed my way of thinking. Something as easy as deciding to have an unoffendable heart can really make a huge difference in your life.

Beginning today, choose to not let others hurt your feelings or offend you. Pray for God to cover your heart and protect it. Let junk your family, friends, or co-workers might toss out slide past you like an egg off a non-stick frying pan. Remember most of the time people step on you without even realizing what they are doing. Get over yourself and don't waste your time wallowing in self-pity while the rest of the world is out having fun. Self-pity is self-punishment. Who needs it? It clearly says in Proverbs 19:11 *"A man's wisdom gives him patience; it is to his glory to overlook an offense."* Overlook it and keep on moving, considering all the not-so-kind words and abrupt or rude actions just irrelevant debris. This is powerful!

God gave dogs an unoffendable heart as standard issue while we have to work at it. Think about it. They seem to understand when you're too busy, they can take criticism and blame without resentment and they can overlook it when they get blamed - even when it wasn't their fault. Anger, bitterness and unforgiveness are just not a part of their lives. Why do we make room for it in ours?

Every once in a while I think about the woman at the retreat who shared the letter-in-the-purse story and it causes me to take inventory. We all should just turn our purses upside down every now and then to see what's in there. We'll be surprised by what we find when we dig around and evaluate the content of our lives, our relationships, and our feelings. Maybe anger is rolling around in the bottom of your heart like a half eaten rock-hard hamburger that needs to hit the trashcan. Or, on the flip side, like finding a forgotten $20 bill hidden in a secret pocket for an emergency, you might realize how blessed you really are. Slowing down long enough to sort it out is what's required. All kinds of things, good and not so good, may surface. Just like cleaning out your purse, in the end when you put back in what really needs to be there, it feels so much better. Scripture reminds us in Philippians: *"And now dear brothers and sisters, one final thing. Fix your thoughts on what is true, and honorable and right, and pure, and lovely, and admirable. Think about things that are excellent and worthy of praise."* That's the kind of stuff we need to be packing.

Chapter 10

When You're Bumped, What Spills Out?

"We are like tea bags – we don't know our strength until we are in hot water."

-Sister Busche

People fascinate me, especially people in church parking lots. One Sunday I arrived early, so I just sat in the car for a minute gathering my thoughts. David dashed out to a meeting an hour before. It was nice to enjoy a calm moment.

An SUV rolled into the lot taking a sudden left turn snatching a parking spot close to the back entrance to the church. The doors flew open and the whole family spilled out. "Daaad. Now I have lipstick half way up my face from your Bat turn. What was that about?" shrieked the teen-aged daughter.

"Stan, look at this mess!" said the wife as she was blotting coffee off her white blouse. "What's wrong with you!

The twelve-year-old son old crawled out with his video game and headset totally unaware.

Another car pulled up with a couple obviously arguing. They were both waiving their hands and shaking their heads. I could tell she was on the brink of tears.

All of a sudden another man walked up to Stan the SUV driver yelling, "What are you thinking man? I was waiting on that spot and you cut right in front of me. My wife still has the cast on her foot and that was the last spot close to the door."

Then I noticed that as our pastor walked out the door to pick up something in his car the whole atmosphere changed. It reminded me of grade school when the teacher left the classroom and all chaos broke out, but the minute she returned everyone was instantly at their best. All the upset churchgoers smiled greeting the pastor like he was the behavior police.

. . . .

It reminded me of grade school when the teacher left the classroom and all chaos broke out, but the minute she returned everyone was instantly at their best.

. . . .

We all have our buttons and when they're hit, we change into strange creatures. It's scary to see what lurks just beneath our shiny surfaces and plastic smiles. We rock along just fine until someone pushes us a little too far then suddenly, without warning, the junk spills out. I hate the thought of the nastiness inside all of us.

I almost threw David into shock the first time he saw someone push one of my buttons. We had been married for about six months. He was a resident director for the student housing where we lived during

106

his last year of college. His responsibility was to make sure everything was secure in the building. At six foot three, David has a commanding presence so he was perfect for the job.

One night we pulled into our building parking lot to find five yelling drunk guys outside the back entrance surrounded by empty beer bottles and cigarette butts. David rolled down the window and we watched like a couple of patrolling cops. At first I was just disgusted, but when the guys began to harass two girls who were trying to go into the building, I felt my anger start to creep to the top. I followed David as he got out of the car and walked to the door causally joining in their conversation. Matter-of-factly he said, "All right guys, it's getting late so we need to pick up these bottles. I've already called the campus shuttle to take you back to where ever you need to go".

One of them said in a mocking, cocky way, "Who are you big guy, the dean of students or something? We don't have to go anywhere."

David calmly started to reason with them when out from behind him I flew landing six inches in front of the offender's face. I said, "Listen tough guy. You and your buddies have about 30 seconds to get your stuff and start walking before all hell breaks loose!"

• •

I said, "Listen tough guy. You and your buddies have about 30 seconds to get your stuff and start walking before all hell breaks loose.!"

• •

I saw that in a movie once and always wanted to try it.

They just stared blankly at me without saying a word. Clearly it caught them off guard when the big guy's little wife in her high heels told them to take a hike or else, because they gathered their stuff and walked toward the shuttle. David turned to me in amazement. Another facet of his complex wife was revealed.

After a somewhat lengthy discussion about safety and procedures, I promised to not risk doing something like that again. There had recently been problems with girls on campus being stalked and David wanted make sure I wasn't one of them.

I did find out something about myself that night. My anger and frustration with those who mistreat women and defy authority rides dangerously close to the surface. So when I was bumped it all spilled out.

Have you ever stopped to consider what pushes your hot button? Everyone has at least one. Some people have several. A friend of mine suggested naming the buttons. If we do, we will have a better understanding of how to control our reactions when they get pushed. It's like we learned in elementary school, practice saying NO! to drugs before they are offered. Being aware of your hot buttons before the get pushed can keep you out of a lot of trouble.

In elementary school I spent a lot of time with my friend, Jonya. Her house always looked picture perfect, like a page out of a magazine. Her mom, Joy, knew how to keep house! She didn't have hired help anyone knew about, but as a little girl I used to imagine she must have a magic wand or something hidden in her pantry. The fairy godmother, Cinderella, and a troop of mice most likely appeared, scrubbed ceiling to floor when Joy waved the wand. Then right before we walked in, the fairy tale crew would scatter and hide back in the pantry. I just knew I was going to catch a glimpse of Cinderella, or at least one of the mice helpers, one day.

Joy loves white. In the living room she had lily-white carpet, a large, soft patterned white sofa, and a shiny white grand piano. On snow days, looking out their living room windows by the piano, it was hard to tell where the outside stopped and the inside started.

As I grew up my Cinderella theory slowly faded when I realized Joy could get away with all white because there weren't any boys in the house, only one grown up very careful man, Jonya's dad. Don't misunderstand me; he's definitely a man's man. He's passionate about all sports, hunts what ever is in season and would probably keep his fishing worms right next to the low fat yogurt in the kitchen refrigerator, but he respected the ladies of the house. I think partly because he was in the minority.

At my house there was my dad, the camp director, and my two older brothers who were always tromping through the house in sweaty athletic shoes and clothes throwing a ball of some sort. Most of the time, at least five of my brothers' friends were there and they were always eating. Mom and I were out numbered eight to two most every day. Our house was not a white carpet house.

At Jonya's house we always had a choice of fruit juices with our snacks. I think Mom had to hide a stash of food and juice so all the boys wouldn't completely wipe out the pantry and refrigerator. It was so different at the Walters' house. The girls always used glasses and didn't drink straight out of the jug ... ever.

Cranberry juice was my favorite. I would always pour a big glass as full as I could. Joy would let us sit in the white room only if we promised to be very careful. I think it was part of our unspoken ladylike training to sit nicely, enjoy a cool beverage and talk quietly. It was good for me because I was clearly more tomboy than ladylike. Knowing this about myself, every time I made that scary walk across the white carpet to the big white fluffy couch I was nothing but focused on my glass.

One afternoon after I found my favorite spot on the couch Jonya and I enjoyed our snacks. We more than likely were deep in discussion about important current events; the cute new boy at school, the heated foursquare game at recess and how mean our teacher was.

I had mastered the art of taking the last bite of cookie and then the last swig of juice so cranberry would be the last thing I tasted. As I reached over to grab the juice while still talking to Jonya, my focus wavered and out flew that last one-ounce sip on to the perfect white, unstained carpet!

I felt like Ralphie in the movie A Christmas Story after he shot his eye with the new Red Rider BB gun. His Mom was forever warning him and then it happened. How could we fix this and fast before we were found out? AHHH! Jonya went straight for the pantry to get the Resolve carpet cleaner. I was really hoping the fairy godmother, who I was sure lived in there, would pop out and say in her British accent, "At your service".

• •

I felt like Ralphie in the movie A Christmas Story after he shot his eye with the new Red Rider BB gun.

• •

I've come to realize we are all filled with something. And just like that glass of juice, we are all going to be bumped because that's life how life runs. We do have a choice in what we fill ourselves up with, either good or bad. What our hearts are full of is what will spill out. Sadly just like the cranberry juice, what spills out often splatters leaving a permanent stain on those around us. Fortunately for me, Joy was full of love and understanding instead of anger and frustration. How we behave under pressure tells more about who we are than anything else.

• •

What our hearts are full of is what will spill out.

• •

Proverbs 27:19 explains this so clearly, "As water reflects a face, so a man's heart reflects the man." What's unnerving to me is people are always watching. Just like the churchgoers in the parking lot who had no idea I was watching their every move, I tend to forget people are watching me every day. I am reminded of the huge responsibility I have to represent the love of God in a consistently authentic way every day. It doesn't work when it's reserved only for when "important" people are watching. I saw that pitiful scene play out in the parking lot. People who don't ever drive into a church parking lot see that kind of flip-flop, confusing behavior and are reminded why they don't bother going to church.

I think life would be less complicated if we were all of more conscious of our hot buttons and what happens when those buttons are bumped. What do we need to be filling ourselves up with? Galatians 5:22-23 spells it out for us. "But the fruit of the Spirit is love, joy, peace, patience, kindness, goodness, faithfulness, gentleness and self-control." If the Spirit of God lives in us, that is what we should be filled up with. So when we are sideswiped or blindsided here's what would splash out:

Love - choosing to give freely of yourself without expecting any return.

Joy - carrying a pair of pompons with you to celebrate life. Don't miss out on a single day, even the tough ones.

Peace – stepping aside and allowing God to run His universe and trusting Him to guide your way.

Patience – not ever giving up. Galatians 6:9 "Let us not get tired of doing good for at the proper time we will reap a harvest, if we do not give up."

Kindness - truly seeing a person as a child of God and treating him or her as such.

Goodness –simply doing what is right even when you don't feel like it. Deuteronomy 6:17 "Do what is right and good in the Lord's sight..."

Faithfulness – being consistently trustworthy and loyal.

Gentleness - life is very fragile so treat people carefully.

Self-Control - disciplining yourself in all circumstances and not allowing the bomb to go off when your buttons are pushed.

Remember the worn out Starbucks kiosk girl in chapter five? The most discouraging part of her story was we were attending a conference hosting several thousand people from the "Christian" community. It breaks my heart to think she might have gone home that day not associating loving, patient, kind, or even remotely nice to the word Christian. It's frightening how much damage can be done by our thoughtless actions.

. . . .

It's frightening how much damage can
be done by our thoughtless actions.

. . . .

In The Book Of Lists the golden retriever is named the least likely to bite and the German shepherd is tagged at the most likely to bite. That is who they are by nature. However, a German shepherd can be trained to be loving and docile just as a golden can be trained to be aggressive and mean. It is encouraging to know, though, we are all trainable - dogs and people. Some of us by nature are just easier to teach.

If we will fill ourselves with love, patience and kindness when life knocks us around, and it will, things that will leave a mark don't even seep out. It's all about awareness and choice. Consider this: Your reactions should be based on your convictions not on your aggravating circumstances.

. . . .

Consider this: Your reactions should be based on your
convictions not on your aggravating circumstances.

. . . .

Learn from the dogs. Life is sweet when we are willing to sit, stay and listen to the Master.

Afterthoughts

We were at lunch with a group of women enjoying girl food and great conversation. Someone asked me about the title of the book we were working on. "Bark Less Wag More," I said, wondering how she would respond.

Smiling, her eyes lit up, "That's a thought provoking title!"

She went on to explain what she had learned from a dog.

"One fall morning, years ago, a mangy mutt showed up at our door. I tried to shoo him away, but he wouldn't leave. Even though I refused to let the boys feed him, he stayed. After several days, he started to grow on us. I found myself feeling sorry for him and began setting table scraps out on the back porch. The boys became attached and as the days grew colder and the bad weather arrived in Ohio, I even brought him in to the laundry room on really cold nights. I don't remember if we ever really gave him an official name.

What I do I remember about the dog, though, was he walked our oldest son, Jeremy, to school and back home every day. In fact, at the end of the school year, the principal gave the dog a perfect attendance certificate at the award's ceremony. But after the assembly, as strangely as he appeared, he disappeared and, much to Jeremy's disappointment, we never saw him again. I've never forgotten his devotion to my son.

I'm sure the dog with no name walked beside my son day in and day out as part protector and part friend. When Jeremy went on the playground in the middle of the day, the dog would be waiting on him, watching over him like a guard. Then he'd be waiting at the end of the day to walk him home – never demanding, never asking for a thing, he was just there. What a companion! I wondered if God brought him just for that very thing – to watch over Jeremy.

That year was Jeremy's first in public school. It was a big change for him from the small private school he'd been attending. Somehow I feel God knew Jeremy needed a special friend for a while. Solomon said, "There is a friend who sticks closer than a brother." So many times I've thought about that dog and how he stuck with Jeremy. Why did he befriend my son? Does God use animals to do His bidding? He owns the cattle on a thousand hills, surely He can work through a street-wise mutt."

God's love for us continually amazes me. He shows His affection and concern in so many wonderful and unusual ways. In return, let's make it a goal to always show abundant love and forgiveness, to become aware of when we need to take time out, to live grateful and kind and, most importantly, to stop whining and enjoy our lives.

Jill Brawner Jones

www.ingramcontent.com/pod-product-compliance
Lightning Source LLC
Chambersburg PA
CBHW060947040426
42445CB00011B/1034